Unlock

the Power of Advanced AI Prompts: A
Complete Guide

ISBN: 979-83-2899-845-1

Embark on a journey to transform your interaction with the digital world.

Prologue

Ever felt stuck staring at a blank page, searching for inspiration, or tangled in technical speak, trying to get your point across? What if you had a magic key to unlock endless creativity and make complex ideas simple? Welcome to the world of AI prompts.

AI prompts, whether from ChatGPT or any AI-driven language model, are your secret weapon to spark creativity, tackle tough tasks, and revolutionize communication. But diving into this world might seem overwhelming. That's where this guide comes in, offering you the tools and tricks to master the art of prompt crafting.

Inside, you'll learn how to communicate effectively with any AI, craft perfect prompts, and unlock the full power of advanced models like GPT-4, now with real-time internet access. You'll be able to tap into the freshest information, get instant updates, and make your interactions with AI even more dynamic and relevant. Imagine having the latest news, weather, and market trends at your fingertips, or brainstorming with up-to-the-minute inspiration. This guide not only teaches you how to use these powerful features but also shows you how they can transform your everyday tasks, enhance your creativity, and supercharge your learning.

This isn't just a learning journey; it's a transformation. AI is about to become your ultimate partner in creativity and clarity. Ready to change how you interact with technology and unleash your potential? Let's get started.

Table of Contents

Prologue

4

Introduction

9

Welcome to the World of ChatGPT Prompts

9

The Power of Effective Prompting

9

Why AI Prompts Matter Today

10

Navigating This Guide

12

Chapter 1:

14

Foundations of AI Communication

14

1.1 Understanding AI and Language Models

14

1.2 The Evolution of Language Models

15

1.3 The Art of Crafting Prompts

17

1.4 Types of Prompts: Open-Ended, Closed-Ended, and Scenario-Based

19

1.5 The Importance of Context and Style

20

1.6 Recognizing Capabilities and Limitations

22

1.7 Understanding GPT-4 and GPT-4o Capabilities

25

1.8 Getting Started with AI: Account Setup and Model Differences

27

Chapter 2:

30

Intermediate Prompt Crafting

30

2.1 The Science of Prompt Engineering

30

2.2 Fine-Tuning Your Prompts for Better Responses

32

2.3 The Magic of Keywords and Specific Instructions

34

2.4 Adapting Writing Styles and Tones

35

2.5 Templates and Boilerplates: Your Best Friends

37

2.6 Leveraging GPT-4's Contextual Understanding

39

2.7 Prompt Engineering Tools and Platforms

41

Chapter 3:

46

Advanced Prompt Crafting Techniques

46

3.1 Specialized Prompts for Every Need

46

3.2 Unleashing Creativity - Prompts for Writers

48

3.3 The Technical Writer's Ally - Generating Documentation

50

3.4 Code Generation - A Programmer's Guide

52

3.5 Analyzing Data with Precision

54

3.6 The Art of Iteration: Refining Your Prompts

56

3.7 Ethical Considerations in the Age of AI

58

3.8 Utilizing GPT-4's Expanded Knowledge Base

61

3.9 Multi-turn Prompt Strategies

63

3.10 Using AI for Multilingual Tasks

65

Chapter 4:

68

Putting It All Into Practice

68

4.1 Case Studies: Real-World Success Stories

68

4.2 Community Wisdom: Learning from Others

70

4.3 Step-by-Step Exercises to Practice Prompt Crafting Skills

73

4.4 Challenge Yourself: Advanced Prompt Scenarios

84

4.5 Adaptive Learning Prompts

91

4.6 Personalized AI Interactions

94

4.7 Collaborative Prompt Crafting

97

4.8 Personal Feedback Integration: Enhancing AI Interactions

100

Chapter 5

103

Advanced Topics:

103

5.1 Exploring Advanced Prompt Design Theories:

103

5.2 Troubleshooting Common Prompt Issues and Getting Better Results

106

5.3 The Future of Prompt Design and Emerging Trends

109

5.4 Ethical Considerations in Using and Advancing LLMs

113

5.5 Exploring GPT-4's Multimodal Capabilities

117

5.6 Interpreting AI Output

121

Chapter 6:

126

Practical Applications and Innovations

126

6.1 Case Studies on GPT-4 Integration

126

6.2 Exploring AI Integrations with IoT

132

Chapter 7

138

Conclusion

138

7.1 The Journey Ahead: Continuing Your AI Exploration

138

7.2 Keeping Up with Advanced Prompt Crafting: Navigating the Continuous Evolution

140

7.3 Future Directions with GPT-4 and Beyond

144

7.4 Building an AI Prompt Portfolio

148

Chapter 8:

151

Bonus AI Unleashed: 20 Key Applications and Expert Strategies for Success

151

8.1 Writing Different Kinds of Creative Content

151

8.2 Answering Your Questions in an Informative Way

153

8.3 Translating Languages: AI as a Multilingual Translator

154

8.4 Summarizing Factual Topics

156

8.5 Creating Different Kinds of Creative Text Formats

158

8.6 Brainstorming Ideas

160

8.7 Debunking Misinformation

162

8.8 Writing Different Kinds of Informal Content

164

8.9 Refactoring Code

166

8.10 Writing Different Kinds of Technical Content

169

8.11 Writing Presentations and Outlines

171

8.12 Bug Fixing in Code

173

8.13 Data Analysis

177

8.14 Generating Different Creative Text Formats

179

8.15 Writing Different Kinds of Lists

181

8.16 Keeping Track of Information

183

8.17 Writing Conversational Scripts

185

8.18 Coming Up with Conversation Starters

187

8.19 Writing Different Kinds of Marketing Copy

189

8.20 Proofreading and Editing Text

191

About the Author

195

Introduction

Welcome to the World of ChatGPT Prompts

Imagine you've just been given a magic lamp. But instead of rubbing it to summon a genie, you communicate your wishes through prompts. This is not fantasy; it's the reality of interacting with advanced AI like ChatGPT. The prompts you craft are your wishes, and how well you articulate them determines the magic you unlock.

In this guide, we're not just going to teach you to make wishes. We're going to show you how to make wishes that ChatGPT can't help but grant in the most helpful ways possible. Whether you're a writer seeking inspiration, a developer needing code, or a business professional looking for market insights, mastering the art of prompt crafting is your key to unlocking a new realm of possibilities.

The Power of Effective Prompting

Prompts are akin to magic spells for AI. A well-crafted prompt can work wonders, yielding exactly the response you need, whether it's to write a captivating story, provide a detailed answer to a complex question, or even generate code for a tricky software problem. But unlike the cryptic incantations of fantasy, the magic of prompts lies in their clarity, precision, and strategic formulation.

Think of AI as a highly skilled but literal-minded assistant. It understands and responds based on the clarity of the instructions it receives. Therefore, crafting an effective prompt isn't just about what you ask but how you ask it. You need to frame your requests in a way that aligns perfectly with the AI's processing patterns. For example, a vague prompt like "Tell me about dogs" can lead to a generic response. However, refining it to "Provide a detailed comparison between the feeding habits of domestic dogs and wolves" directs the AI to generate a focused and informative answer.

As we dive deeper into this guide, we'll start with the fundamental principles of prompt engineering. You'll learn the importance of specificity and how different types of prompts—such as open-ended, closed-ended, and scenario-based—can drastically alter the AI's output. We'll explore techniques to refine your prompting skills, from adjusting the level of detail in your questions to leveraging the model's latest features for nuanced responses.

Moreover, effective prompting also involves a dynamic interaction with AI. It's about iterating on your prompts based on the responses you receive, fine-tuning your approach, and understanding the subtleties of how AI interprets and processes your inputs. This iterative cycle helps in honing your ability to wield this powerful tool, ensuring that you achieve not just acceptable, but fantastic results.

So, let's embark on this journey together to unlock the full potential of your interactions with AI. By mastering the art of the prompt, you will be equipped to command this digital sorcery, harnessing the capabilities of AI to meet your needs precisely and effectively. Whether you are looking to inspire creativity, solve practical problems, or innovate in ways yet imagined, understanding and mastering the power of effective prompting is your first step towards success.

Why AI Prompts Matter Today

In today's digital age, AI is intricately woven into the fabric of our daily lives, influencing how we shop, the media we consume, and the way businesses operate and engage with customers. The invisible hand of AI can be seen in personalized marketing emails, the recommendations on streaming platforms, or even in the intelligent assistants that simplify our day-to-day tasks. As these technologies become more pervasive, the ability to interact with AI effectively transforms from a mere skill to an essential capability.

The significance of AI prompting extends across various sectors. In healthcare, for instance, AI helps manage patient data, assists in diagnostic processes, and supports research into new treatments. Effective prompts can enhance these applications, making AI tools more accurate and responsive to the specific needs of healthcare professionals and patients. Similarly, in finance, AI analyzes vast amounts of data for investment insights, risk assessment, and fraud prevention. Here, well-crafted prompts are crucial for extracting precise information and making informed decisions.

In the educational sector, AI's role is rapidly expanding. From personalized learning environments that adapt to the pace and style of individual learners to automated grading systems and virtual tutors, AI enhances the educational experience. Effective prompting ensures that the AI's interactions are beneficial, encouraging, and tailored to improve learning outcomes.

Moreover, in the entertainment industry, AI is reshaping content creation, from music and video games to films and virtual reality experiences. Prompts that guide AI in generating creative and engaging content can lead to innovative storytelling and new forms of interactive media.

This guide aims not only to teach you the mechanics of crafting effective prompts but also to underscore why these skills are increasingly valuable. As AI technologies evolve and their applications broaden, the ability to communicate effectively with AI will be critical. Those who master this skill will be better equipped to leverage AI's capabilities, lead innovation, and solve complex problems in real-world settings.

By understanding the strategic importance of AI prompting, you'll be able to see the tangible benefits it brings to professional and personal arenas. Whether you're looking to enhance productivity, foster creativity, or drive technological adoption, effective AI prompting is a key that unlocks vast potential. This guide will provide you with the knowledge and tools necessary to excel in this dynamic field, ensuring you are prepared for the future as AI continues to transform the world.

Navigating This Guide

We've carefully structured this guide to be as friendly and accessible as possible. Each chapter is designed to build on the last, creating a smooth progression that takes you from the foundational basics right through to more advanced techniques. Our goal is to transform what might initially appear as complex and intimidating into something approachable and manageable.

By breaking down intricate ideas into understandable steps, we not only make learning more straightforward but also more engaging. Throughout the guide, you'll find we've peppered our explanations with practical examples and personal anecdotes. These serve multiple purposes: they illuminate the real-world applications of what you're learning, they help demystify the more challenging aspects of AI prompts, and they make the technical content more relatable.

For instance, in our discussion on crafting effective prompts, we won't just tell you how to do it; we'll show you. You'll read stories about how specific prompts have been used to solve actual problems, like a business improving its customer service or a writer overcoming writer's block. These stories not only illustrate the potential of AI prompts but also encourage you to think creatively about how you can apply these techniques in your own life or work.

As you move through the guide, you'll notice that each chapter incrementally introduces more sophisticated concepts and practices. This is intentional, ensuring that you're never overwhelmed but always building on a solid foundation of knowledge. From the simplest tasks to the nuances of prompt engineering for complex AI applications, we guide you step-by-step.

Ready to start your journey into the world of AI prompts? Let's dive in! With this guide as your companion, you're well-equipped to explore the capabilities of AI like never before. Each section sets the stage for a comprehensive exploration of ChatGPT prompts, ensuring that readers of all levels—whether you're a novice just starting out or an experienced user looking to refine your skills—feel welcomed and prepared to delve deeper into the fascinating subject matter. Let's embark on this transformative journey together, unlocking the full potential of what AI can achieve with the right prompts.

Chapter 1:

Foundations of AI Communication

1.1 Understanding AI and Language Models

So, what exactly is AI? At its core, Artificial Intelligence (AI) is a broad field of computer science focused on creating smart machines capable of performing tasks that typically require human intelligence. These tasks can include recognizing speech, making decisions, translating between languages, and, as you'll see with models like GPT-4, understanding and generating human language.

AI is often discussed in terms of its ability to mimic or even enhance human capabilities. For instance, when we talk about AI in everyday technology, it's usually in the context of software that predicts what you'll type next in your email, what you might want to watch on TV, or how you might best route your drive home to avoid traffic.

Language Models: GPT-4, which stands at the forefront of this technology, is a type of AI known as a language model. Developed by OpenAI, GPT-4 (Generative Pre-trained Transformer 4) represents the cutting edge of neural networks specialized in language tasks. These models are "pre-trained" on vast amounts of text from the internet, books, articles, and more. This pre-training allows them to understand and generate human-like text based on the input (or "prompt") they receive.

But how does this work in practice? Think of GPT-4 as a highly advanced version of predictive text. It looks at the words you give it and predicts what comes next, not just one word at a time but whole paragraphs of coherent and contextually appropriate content. This capability doesn't just mimic understanding; when done well, it can seem like the AI truly grasps the conversation.

Effective Communication with AI: Communicating effectively with GPT-4, therefore, means more than just typing out a question or a command. It involves understanding how the model generates its responses. When you know the basics of how these models are trained and how they operate, you can craft prompts that play to their strengths and avoid their weaknesses. For example, GPT-4 can generate impressively detailed responses about well-documented topics, but it might struggle with extremely niche or newly emerging topics that have limited documentation.

In this chapter, we're going to explore the fundamentals of how AI like GPT-4 processes language and how you can leverage this understanding to communicate your ideas more effectively. Whether you're looking to generate creative writing, pull insights from data, or automate customer service interactions, knowing the underlying principles of AI and language models is your first step towards mastery.

1.2 The Evolution of Language Models

The field of language models has witnessed a remarkable evolution, shaping how machines understand and interact with human language. This journey through the development of language models not only highlights the strides made in AI technology but also sets the stage for the sophisticated capabilities of modern models like GPT-4.

Early Beginnings: The genesis of language models can be traced back to simpler statistical methods, where the models would predict subsequent words based on the frequency and pattern of words in a given dataset. These early models, such as n-gram models, were limited by their reliance on the immediate context (usually just a few preceding words), lacking a deeper, semantic understanding of text.

Transition to Neural Networks: The introduction of neural networks marked a significant shift in this field. Unlike their predecessors, neural networks, particularly Recurrent Neural Networks (RNNs) and later Long Short-Term Memory networks (LSTMs), could remember longer sequences of text, making them better at understanding context and generating more coherent passages of text. However, they were still often hampered by issues like gradient vanishing, where they would lose track of very long input sequences.

The Rise of Transformers: The real breakthrough came with the development of the Transformer architecture, introduced in the paper "Attention is All You Need" by Vaswani et al. in 2017. Transformers revolutionized language understanding by using mechanisms called attention and self-attention, allowing the model to weigh the importance of different words in a sentence or a document, regardless of their position. This architecture enabled models to have a much better understanding of context and nuance.

From BERT to GPT-4: Building on the Transformer architecture, models like BERT (Bidirectional Encoder Representations from Transformers) and GPT (Generative Pre-trained Transformer) series began to emerge. BERT improved understanding by analyzing text in both directions (left-to-right and right-to-left), while GPT focused on generating predictive text in a coherent and contextually relevant manner. GPT-4, the latest in this series, has been trained on a diverse range of internet text and fine-tuned through advanced techniques, making it one of the most powerful language models to date.

Capabilities of GPT-4: With its extensive training and sophisticated architecture, GPT-4 can generate text that is not only contextually accurate but also nuanced and surprisingly deep. It understands and generates multiple languages, crafts poetry, codes in several programming languages, and much more, often performing at or above human levels in specific tasks.

Implications for AI Communication: The evolution of language models from simple statistical frameworks to complex neural architectures like GPT-4 illustrates significant growth in AI's ability to process and generate human language. This advancement is crucial for anyone looking to harness AI for tasks ranging from automated customer service to creative writing and technical documentation.

As we delve deeper into how these models work and how to interact with them, it's important to appreciate the technological heritage that has enabled such capabilities. Understanding this evolution helps us not only in crafting better prompts but also in foreseeing where the technology might head next, preparing us for future innovations in AI communication.

1.3 The Art of Crafting Prompts

Crafting a good prompt is much like asking a question in just the right way—it's about clarity, specificity, and understanding the capabilities of the AI you're communicating with. When you master the art of prompt crafting, you turn simple interactions into powerful tools for generating useful and insightful responses. Let's explore the essentials of crafting effective prompts and see how with some straightforward examples, you can enhance the quality of your interactions with AI.

Clarity and Specificity: The first rule of thumb is to be as clear and specific as possible. Vague prompts often lead to vague responses. For instance, if you ask GPT-4, "Tell me about London," the model might provide a generic overview of the city. However, if you refine the prompt to, "What are the top five historical sites to visit in London as of 2024?" you guide the AI to generate a much more specific and useful response.

Understanding the Model's Capabilities: It's crucial to align your prompts with what the AI is capable of handling. GPT-4, with its vast training data, is adept at handling a wide range of topics. However, its responses are limited to its training data up until its last update. Asking it about very recent events or expecting real-time updates can lead to outdated or inaccurate information. Therefore, tailor your prompts to the strengths of the model—such as historical data analysis, creative writing, or technical explanations.

Using the Right Structure: The structure of your prompt can significantly impact the response. For example, open-ended prompts encourage the model to generate more creative and expansive answers, while closed-ended prompts are useful for obtaining specific, concise information. Scenario-based prompts, where you set up a situation and ask the model to respond within that context, can be particularly effective for complex interactions.

Example Prompts:

Open-ended: "Write a short story about a detective solving a mystery in Paris."
Closed-ended: "Is Paris the capital of France?"
Scenario-based: "Imagine you are a tour guide in Paris. Describe a day tour itinerary that includes historical sites and gourmet dining."

Iterative Prompting: Another effective strategy is iterative prompting, where you start with a broad prompt and gradually narrow down based on the AI's responses. This method is particularly useful when exploring topics where your initial knowledge is limited. For example:
Start with: "What are the major causes of climate change?"
Follow up based on the response: "How does deforestation contribute to climate change?"
Further refine: "What are the current rates of deforestation globally?"

Feedback and Refinement: As you interact more with the AI, take note of which prompts yield the most satisfactory answers. Refining your prompts based on previous interactions can greatly improve the quality of future responses. This ongoing feedback loop not only enhances your prompt crafting skills but also deepens your understanding of how AI models process and generate language.

By adhering to these guidelines and regularly practicing your prompt crafting skills, you'll find that your ability to communicate effectively with AI will grow exponentially. The better your prompts, the better the AI's responses will be, allowing you to leverage the full capabilities of advanced language models like GPT-4 for any task at hand.

1.4 Types of Prompts: Open-Ended, Closed-Ended, and Scenario-Based

Understanding the different types of prompts is crucial in harnessing the full potential of AI communication. Each type of prompt serves a unique purpose and can be tailored to achieve specific kinds of responses. Let's delve into the three primary types: open-ended, closed-ended, and scenario-based prompts, providing clear examples of each to illustrate their uses.

Open-Ended Prompts: Open-ended prompts are designed to elicit a detailed or creative response. They do not restrict the AI's output to a specific format or answer, allowing for a wide range of possible responses. This type of prompt is particularly useful for brainstorming, creative writing, or exploring complex topics where multiple viewpoints or ideas are beneficial.

Example: "Discuss the impact of renewable energy on global economies."

AI Response: The AI might elaborate on various impacts, such as job creation in new sectors, the reduction of carbon footprints, or the economic challenges of transitioning from fossil fuels. The response could cover multiple aspects, providing a rich, multifaceted perspective.

Closed-Ended Prompts: Closed-ended prompts are designed to receive a precise, often short answer. These are particularly useful when you need specific information or when the response does not require elaboration. Such prompts help in obtaining facts, making decisions based on binary (yes/no) answers, or when compiling data that require straightforward responses.

Example: "Is solar power cost-effective compared to coal as of 2024?"

AI Response: The AI might respond with a simple "Yes" or "No," possibly followed by a brief explanation or comparison based on current data, summarizing cost-efficiency in terms of installation, maintenance, and output.

Scenario-Based Prompts: Scenario-based prompts involve setting up a context or scenario for the AI to respond within. This type of prompt is highly effective for simulations, role-play situations, or any task where contextual creativity or decision-making is required. It allows the AI to showcase its understanding of nuances in varied situations.

Example: "Imagine you are a travel agent. A client wants a two-week vacation plan for a family of four to Japan, focusing on cultural experiences and nature. What itinerary would you suggest?"

AI Response: The AI, acting as a travel agent, would craft a detailed travel plan including flights, accommodations, and a day-by-day schedule of activities that emphasize cultural sites, such as temples and museums, as well as natural attractions like Mount Fuji or Nara Park.

By choosing the right type of prompt for your needs, you can greatly enhance the effectiveness of your interactions with AI. Open-ended prompts allow for depth and breadth in responses, closed-ended prompts provide succinct and specific information, and scenario-based prompts offer detailed and contextually relevant answers. Understanding and applying these types in your AI communications will not only improve the quality of responses you receive but also increase the efficiency of your tasks, whether for personal use, academic purposes, or professional projects.

1.5 The Importance of Context and Style

Context is key! This phrase cannot be overstated when it comes to interacting with AI, especially sophisticated language models like GPT-4. The more context you provide in your prompts, the better and more accurate the responses you'll receive. In addition to context, the style of your prompts also plays a crucial role in shaping the AI's output. Let's delve into how you can master both these elements to enhance your interactions with AI.

Understanding Context: Context in a prompt helps the AI understand the "why" and the "how" behind your question, enabling it to generate more relevant and targeted responses. Without sufficient context, AI responses can be generic or off-target, as the model may not grasp the nuances or specific focus of your inquiry.

Example: Asking "How do I fix an error?" is vague and likely to result in a broad, unhelpful answer. However, providing context such as, "I'm coding in Python and encountered a 'SyntaxError: unexpected EOF while parsing'. What does this mean and how can I fix it?" gives the AI clear information about the programming language, the specific error, and your need for a solution. This context leads to a precise and actionable response.

Choosing the Right Style: The style of your prompt should match the intended purpose and audience of the AI's response. Style can include the tone (formal or informal), complexity of language (simplified or technical), and the format of the response (bullet points, detailed paragraph, etc.)

Example: If you're a teacher asking AI to generate a quiz for students, the style should be educational and straightforward. A prompt like, "Create a 10-question quiz on photosynthesis for 8th-grade students, with multiple-choice answers," specifies the educational level, subject matter, and format, guiding the AI to produce content that is suitable for middle school students.

Incorporating Context and Style in Prompts:

1. **Identify the purpose of your interaction.** Are you seeking information, creating content, solving a problem, or something else?
2. **Determine the necessary details** that need to be included to make the AI's task clear. Specify any relevant conditions, constraints, or preferences.
3. **Decide on the appropriate style** based on who will use or view the AI's output. Consider the tone, complexity, and format that best suit the end user.
4. **Craft your prompt** by integrating all these elements. A well-composed prompt reduces ambiguity and enhances the effectiveness of the response.

Example: For a business executive, a prompt might be, "Draft an email to our clients explaining the delay in project delivery due to supply chain issues. Keep the tone professional and empathetic, summarize the reasons, and assure them of our commitment to resolving the situation."

By giving the right context and choosing an appropriate style, you turn simple interactions into powerful exchanges that produce valuable and specific outcomes. These skills are essential for anyone looking to leverage AI effectively, whether for personal use, educational purposes, or professional projects. As we progress through this guide, you'll see more examples and techniques on setting context and style, helping you to become proficient in crafting prompts that get the best possible responses from AI.

1.6 Recognizing Capabilities and Limitations

GPT-4 is a cutting-edge tool in artificial intelligence, significantly enhancing how we interact with information and automate complex tasks. However, while it's crucial to leverage GPT-4's robust capabilities, it's equally important to understand its limitations. Acknowledging both aspects will ensure more effective use and help set realistic expectations.

Capabilities of GPT-4:

GPT-4's training on a diverse and extensive dataset enables it to handle a broad range of topics with considerable fluency and coherence. Here's a breakdown of its key strengths:

1. **Language Understanding and Generation:**

Multilingual Proficiency: GPT-4 can understand and generate text in multiple languages, facilitating translation, content creation, and global communication.

Advanced Contextual Comprehension: It excels in generating relevant and detailed responses by understanding the nuanced context of queries.

2. Complex Problem Solving:

Analytical Prowess: The model can assist in solving intricate problems across various domains, including mathematics, strategic planning, and logical reasoning.

Data Analysis: GPT-4 can interpret large volumes of data, providing insights and actionable summaries that aid decision-making.

3. Content Creation:

Creative and Technical Writing: From composing narratives and articles to generating technical documents and reports, GPT-4 can adapt its writing to match specific genres or styles.

Educational Content: It is capable of assisting with educational material, offering explanations and creating learning aids across academic fields.

4. Real-Time Information Access:

Live Data Retrieval: Unlike previous models, GPT-4 can access up-to-date information by fetching data from external sources in real-time. This ability enhances its utility for applications requiring current data.

Limitations of GPT-4:

Despite these advancements, GPT-4 has limitations that must be considered:

1. Dependence on Data Sources:

Reliability of Information: While GPT-4 can now access live data, the accuracy of the information depends on the reliability of the sources it uses. Users should verify data independently, especially for critical decision-making.

Static Knowledge Base: For topics not covered by real-time updates, GPT-4's knowledge remains as recent as the last training update, which may not include the very latest developments.

2. Understanding Context and Nuance:

Subtleties and Ambiguity: GPT-4 might still miss subtle nuances of context or misinterpret the intent behind complex queries, which could lead to less relevant responses.

3. Inherent AI Biases:

Bias and Fairness: As with any AI trained on internet data, GPT-4 may reflect and perpetuate biases present in its training material, potentially impacting the fairness and neutrality of its responses.

4. Creativity and Innovation Limits:

Pattern-Based Outputs: GPT-4's creativity is derived from learned data patterns; it cannot originate completely new ideas or theories beyond what it has been trained on.

5. Ethical and Regulatory Challenges:

Data Privacy and Compliance: Users must navigate ethical considerations around data privacy and ensure that their use of GPT-4 adheres to applicable laws, especially in sensitive fields such as healthcare and finance.

Practical Examples:

Effective Use: Utilizing GPT-4 to ask, "What are the latest trends in renewable energy?" can now provide current insights, assuming reliable data sources are accessible.

Limitations in Action: Inquiring about "Recent scientific discoveries in astrophysics" may still yield outdated information if the latest findings haven't been incorporated into accessible databases or are outside the scope of the model's real-time data access.

Understanding the capabilities and limitations of GPT-4 enables users to tailor their prompts effectively, maximize the AI's strengths, and critically assess its output. This balanced approach not only enhances productivity but also ensures a responsible and ethical utilization of the technology. As we continue exploring what GPT-4 can do, keeping these considerations in mind will allow us to harness its power effectively and responsibly.

1.7 Understanding GPT-4 and GPT-4o Capabilities

GPT-4 and its optimized counterpart, GPT-4o, introduce an array of new features that significantly build upon the capabilities of previous models. These advancements not only enhance the overall performance and usability of the AI but also equip users with more robust tools for crafting effective prompts. Let's delve into the improvements these models offer and how they can enhance your AI interactions.

Enhanced Contextual Understanding: A key upgrade in GPT-4 and GPT-4o is their enhanced ability to grasp and maintain context over extended interactions. This advancement means the AI can manage more complex queries and sustain coherence throughout multi-turn conversations, yielding more relevant and accurate responses.

Example: When you craft a prompt for a complex report involving multiple sections and subsections, GPT-4 and GPT-4o can track the overarching structure and context, resulting in a unified and coherent output.

Greater Precision and Fluency: Both models have received significant enhancements in their language generation capabilities. They now produce text with greater precision and fluency, mimicking human-like writing styles more effectively and reducing instances of awkward phrasing.

Example: If you require the AI to draft an email or compose a creative piece, the improved fluency ensures the output is polished and professional, minimizing grammatical errors and awkward constructions.

Advanced Data Access: Particularly with GPT-4o, there is an introduction of advanced data access capabilities, allowing the AI to pull real-time information from the web. This feature is invaluable for tasks that depend on the latest data or insights.

Example: When inquiring about the latest technological trends or recent news events, GPT-4o can access up-to-date information, ensuring that the responses are both relevant and timely.

Improved Task-Specific Performance: The latest models have been fine-tuned to perform better across a variety of specific tasks, from coding and technical documentation to creative storytelling and data analysis. This specialization means the AI can handle specialized prompts with greater effectiveness.

Example: For developers, prompting GPT-4o to debug a piece of code or generate a script will produce more accurate and functional outcomes than previous iterations.

Customizable Output: GPT-4 and GPT-4o offer increased flexibility in customizing the tone, style, and format of the responses. This adaptability allows you to tailor the AI's output to suit specific needs, whether you need a formal report, a casual blog post, or a detailed technical document.

Example: When composing a business proposal, you can dictate the level of formality and detail required, and the AI will adjust its writing style accordingly to meet the stipulated standards.

Multimodal Capabilities: Both GPT-4 and particularly GPT-4o have enhanced multimodal capabilities, meaning they can process and generate responses not only from text but also from other data types like images. This broadens the potential applications of the AI considerably.

Example: You can prompt GPT-4o to generate descriptive text based on an image or provide insights from a graph or chart, making it a versatile tool for various multimedia projects.

Ethical and Safe Use: Both models come equipped with improved mechanisms for ethical and safe use, enhancing the handling of sensitive topics and reducing the potential for harmful biases in the content generated. These improvements are critical for maintaining the trust and integrity of AI interactions.

Example: When engaging the AI in discussions about sensitive social issues, the enhanced ethical frameworks ensure that the responses are more balanced and responsible, minimizing the risk of perpetuating biases or misinformation.

By understanding and utilizing these new features, you can craft more effective prompts that fully leverage the capabilities of GPT-4 and GPT-4o. Whether your goal is to generate high-quality content, access the latest information, or create sophisticated interactive experiences, these models provide the tools and flexibility needed to achieve your objectives effectively.

1.8 Getting Started with AI: Account Setup and Model Differences

Before diving into the world of AI prompts, it's essential to understand how to get started with AI tools like ChatGPT and the differences between various AI models. This section will guide you through the process of creating an account and explain the key distinctions between models to help you choose the right one for your needs.

Creating an Account:

1. Visit the OpenAI Website:
Go to the https://openai.com/

2. Sign Up:
Click on the "Sign Up" button and fill in your details. You may need to provide an email address and create a password.

3. Verify Your Email:

Check your email for a verification link from OpenAI and click on it to verify your account.

4. Choose a Subscription Plan:

OpenAI offers different subscription plans, including free and paid options. Choose the plan that best suits your needs and budget.

5. Access the AI Model:

Once your account is set up and verified, you can log in and start using the AI models available under your subscription plan.

Understanding Different AI Models:

1. GPT-3 vs. GPT-4:

GPT-3: A powerful language model known for its ability to generate human-like text based on the prompts it receives. It's widely used for various applications, from content creation to coding assistance.

GPT-4: The latest iteration, offering enhanced capabilities, including real-time internet access for up-to-date information retrieval. It provides more accurate, relevant, and dynamic responses.

2. Capabilities and Use Cases:

Basic Models: Suitable for general text generation tasks, simple queries, and creative writing. Ideal for users who need a reliable tool for everyday tasks.

Advanced Models (e.g., GPT-4): Best for tasks requiring real-time information, complex problem-solving, and detailed data analysis. These models are equipped to handle more sophisticated applications and deliver high-quality, current results.

3. Customization and Fine-Tuning:

Customization: Both models can be customized to better suit specific needs. Users can fine-tune prompts to get more accurate and tailored responses.

Fine-Tuning: Advanced users can train the models on specific datasets to improve performance in niche areas, making the AI more effective for specialized tasks.

Conclusion: Setting up an account and understanding the differences between AI models are crucial first steps in your journey with AI prompts. By choosing the right model and subscription plan, you can optimize your interactions and make the most of the powerful capabilities these tools offer. With this foundation, you'll be well-prepared to dive into the detailed strategies and techniques covered in this guide.

Chapter 2:

Intermediate Prompt Crafting

2.1 The Science of Prompt Engineering

Having mastered the basics, let's delve deeper into the science of creating effective prompts. Prompt engineering is a strategic and nuanced skill essential for eliciting precise and relevant responses from AI. This chapter will explore techniques that refine your prompts, enhancing the quality and utility of the AI's outputs.

Understanding the Objective: The cornerstone of effective prompt engineering is a clear understanding of your interaction's objective with the AI. Whether you're gathering information, generating content, or solving a problem, a well-defined goal will steer the content and structure of your prompt.

Example: If your objective is to compose a technical article, your prompt should succinctly outline the specific elements of the topic you need covered, like "Explain the principles of quantum computing, including key algorithms and real-world applications."

Precision and Clarity: Clarity and precision are paramount in crafting effective prompts. Ambiguous or overly broad questions often yield vague responses. Specify what you need from the AI, detailing any particular aspects or constraints relevant to your query.

Example: Instead of a general inquiry such as "Tell me about machine learning," opt for a more targeted prompt: "Describe the differences between supervised and unsupervised machine learning, including examples of each."

Incorporating Context: Adding context to your prompts helps the AI grasp the specifics and background of your request. This might include details about the intended audience, the purpose of the response, or pertinent previous interactions.

Example: To obtain a response tailored for a specific audience, you could ask, "Write a blog post about the benefits of renewable energy for high school students, focusing on how solar and wind energy function."

Using Structured Prompts: Structured prompts outline the desired format or the key points the AI should address. This is especially useful for complex requests or when the response must follow a particular structure.

Example: "Create a project plan for developing a mobile app, detailing project objectives, key milestones, required resources, and potential challenges."

Iterative Refinement: Prompt engineering often involves iterative refinement. Start with a basic prompt and progressively refine it based on the AI's responses to achieve more accurate and valuable outputs.

Example: Begin with a general inquiry, "How can businesses benefit from AI?" and refine it to more specific applications, "How can small businesses utilize AI for enhancing customer service and data analysis?"

Using Examples and Comparisons: Incorporating examples or requesting comparisons can clarify your needs and elicit more focused responses. This approach is particularly effective for explanatory or comparative tasks.

Example: "Explain the difference between data mining and data warehousing, providing examples of tools used for each."

Leveraging Keywords and Phrases: Embedding specific keywords and phrases in your prompts can direct the AI's attention and enhance the relevance of its responses. Choose terms that are directly related to the information you seek.

Example: "Summarize recent advancements in natural language processing, focusing on transformer models and their applications."

Avoiding Common Pitfalls: Be mindful of common pitfalls such as leading questions, overly intricate prompts, or insufficient specificity, which can lead to biased, confusing, or irrelevant responses.

Example: Rather than asking a complex question like, "What are the advantages and disadvantages of various renewable energy sources, considering factors like cost, efficiency, environmental impact, and scalability, particularly in urban versus rural settings?" break it into more digestible, focused prompts.

By mastering these techniques, you will enhance your ability to craft precise, relevant prompts that yield high-quality responses from GPT-4 and GPT-4o. As you refine your prompt engineering skills, your interactions with AI will become increasingly effective and insightful, helping you achieve your objectives with greater efficiency and accuracy.

2.2 Fine-Tuning Your Prompts for Better Responses

Sometimes, the difference between an adequate response and an exceptional one comes down to small adjustments in how you phrase your prompts. Fine-tuning your prompts can significantly enhance the quality of the responses you receive from AI. This section will guide you through the process of refining your prompts to achieve the best possible outcomes.

Assessing Initial Responses: Start by evaluating the initial responses you receive from the AI. Identify areas where the response might be lacking in detail, clarity, or relevance. This assessment will help you pinpoint what needs to be adjusted in your prompt.

Example: If the response to "Tell me about the history of the internet" is too general, you might specify, "Describe the key developments in the history of the internet from the 1990s to the present."

Adding Specificity: One of the most effective ways to enhance your prompts is by adding specificity. Clarifying the exact information or type of response you seek guides the AI more directly and can lead to more targeted and useful outputs.

Example: Change a broad prompt like, "How do companies use big data?" to a more specific one, "What are the top three ways in which tech startups have used big data to improve customer experience?"

Clarifying the Context: Context is crucial for guiding the AI's understanding of your prompt. Provide background information, define the scope of the query, or set the scene more vividly to help the AI generate more relevant responses.

Example: Instead of saying, "Write a proposal," specify, "Draft a proposal for a grant aimed at funding community gardens in urban areas, focusing on environmental benefits and community engagement."

Refining Language and Tone: Adjusting the language and tone of your prompts can also influence the responses. Decide whether a formal, technical, conversational, or playful tone is most appropriate for your needs and tailor your prompt accordingly.

Example: For a business report, ensure your prompt conveys a formal tone, "Prepare a detailed market analysis report for the renewable energy sector in Europe, highlighting growth trends and key players."

Incorporating Feedback Loops: Use feedback loops to refine your prompts based on the responses you get. If a response doesn't meet your expectations, tweak the prompt slightly and resend it. This iterative process helps you home in on the most effective way to communicate your query.

Example: If the response to your prompt about solar energy advancements is unsatisfactory, you might refine it to, "Provide an analysis of the latest technological advancements in solar energy and their commercial viability over the last five years."

Testing Different Formats: Experiment with different formats to see which elicits the best response. You might try bullet points, questions, or directive statements to frame your prompt differently.

Example: Instead of a narrative prompt, try listing questions: "What is the current cost of solar panels? How has this changed over the last decade? What factors have influenced price changes?"

By fine-tuning your prompts—through specificity, context clarification, tone adjustment, and continuous refinement—you can dramatically improve the responses from AI. These subtle yet powerful adjustments ensure that you receive more precise, relevant, and actionable answers, helping you make the most of your AI interactions.

2.3 The Magic of Keywords and Specific Instructions

Keywords and specific instructions can act like magic words in the realm of AI interactions, guiding the AI to deliver precisely what you're looking for. This powerful approach ensures that your prompts are not only clear and directed but also highly effective in eliciting the desired response. This section will explore how to harness the potential of keywords and precise instructions to optimize your interactions with AI.

Identifying Effective Keywords: Choosing the right keywords is crucial for directing the AI's focus. Keywords should be relevant to the topic you're exploring and specific enough to guide the AI towards the desired subject matter without ambiguity.

Example: For financial analysis, keywords like "market trends," "investment returns," "sector growth," and "economic indicators" can steer the AI toward a more analytical and data-driven response.

Incorporating Keywords into Prompts: Once you've identified the right keywords, the next step is to seamlessly integrate them into your prompts. This integration should feel natural and should clearly indicate the focus of your query.

Example: Instead of a vague prompt like, "Tell me about the latest in AI technology," refine it to, "Summarize recent advancements in AI technology focusing on machine learning algorithms, natural language processing, and robotics."

Using Specific Instructions: Beyond keywords, specific instructions play a crucial role in shaping the AI's output. These instructions can dictate the format, detail, scope, and perspective of the response.

Example: "Write a detailed comparison of the latest models of electric cars from Tesla and Nissan, highlighting cost, battery life, and user reviews. Provide a summary table with key specifications."

Balancing Keywords and Natural Language: While keywords are powerful, your prompts should also maintain natural language flow to ensure clarity. The AI needs to understand the context in which keywords are used, not just the keywords themselves.

Example: Rather than stuffing a prompt with keywords, such as "Finance, stocks, bonds, market analysis," a more effective prompt would be, "Provide a detailed market analysis of current trends in stocks and bonds."

Avoiding Keyword Stuffing: It's important to use keywords judiciously. Overloading a prompt with keywords can confuse the AI and lead to garbled or overly generic responses.

Example: Instead of "Smartphone, battery, screen, price, camera quality, review," use "Review the latest smartphones focusing on battery life, screen quality, camera capabilities, and price."

Adjusting Keywords Based on Responses: If the initial response doesn't meet your expectations, consider adjusting the keywords or the way they are presented in the prompt. This tweaking can often realign the AI's responses with your actual needs.

Example: If a prompt like "Discuss the impacts of climate change on global agriculture" yields too broad a response, refine it to, "Analyze the effects of climate change on crop yields and farming practices in Southeast Asia."

By effectively using keywords and specific instructions, you can dramatically enhance the precision and relevancy of the AI's responses. This strategic approach not only streamlines the interaction but also ensures that the outputs are directly aligned with your informational needs and objectives.

2.4 Adapting Writing Styles and Tones

The ability to adapt the writing style and tone of the AI's output is crucial for ensuring that the content meets the specific needs of your audience or the requirements of your project. Whether you need a formal tone for a business report or a casual tone for a blog post, understanding how to direct the AI appropriately is key. This section will guide you on how to adjust the AI's writing style to match your needs effectively.

Understanding Style and Tone: First, it's important to distinguish between style and tone. Style refers to the overall approach to writing, which can include the structure, vocabulary, and level of formality. Tone, on the other hand, conveys the writer's attitude towards the subject or the audience, such as serious, playful, formal, or informal.

Example: For a legal document, you might choose a formal style with complex sentences and technical language, and a serious tone to reflect the gravity of the content.

Specifying Style and Tone in Prompts: To get the desired style and tone from the AI, your prompts need to be explicit about your requirements. Clearly articulate not only the content but also how you want that content to be presented.

Example: "Draft a client-facing proposal for a new product launch, using a formal style with persuasive language to emphasize benefits and ROI."

Using Examples to Guide Style: One effective way to ensure you achieve the desired style and tone is to provide the AI with examples of what you're looking for. This can be a reference to a well-known writing style or previous content that matches your desired approach.

Example: "Generate a product review similar in style and tone to reviews found on The Verge, focusing on user experience and technical specifications."

Adjusting Based on Feedback: Once you receive the initial output from the AI, it might be necessary to fine-tune the style and tone. Provide specific feedback on what needs to change to better match your expectations.

Example: If the tone is too formal for a casual audience, you might revise your instruction: "Rewrite the article in a conversational tone, using everyday language and humor to engage young readers."

Consistency Across Multiple Texts: If you're producing a series of texts, maintaining consistency in style and tone is crucial. Make sure to specify this requirement in your prompts to avoid variations that could confuse your audience.

Example: "Create a series of blog posts on health and wellness for college students, maintaining a consistent, informal tone and style that is engaging and relatable across all articles."

Leveraging AI Capabilities for Style Adaptation: Take advantage of the AI's advanced capabilities to mimic different writing styles and tones. Explicitly state if you want the content to emulate the style of a particular writer, genre, or publication.

Example: "Compose an email to our customers about the upcoming product update, mimicking the empathetic and reassuring tone used by our CEO in company-wide communications."

By mastering the ability to adjust the AI's writing style and tone, you can ensure that each piece of content not only delivers the right message but also resonates with the intended audience in the most effective way. This skill is essential for tailoring communications to suit different contexts, audiences, and purposes.

2.5 Templates and Boilerplates: Your Best Friends

Templates and boilerplates are invaluable tools in prompt crafting, particularly when you need to produce consistent and high-quality content efficiently. By using templates, you can save significant time and effort, ensuring that each piece of content adheres to a certain standard and style without having to start from scratch every time. This section will introduce you to the concept of templates and boilerplates and show you how to customize them for various tasks.

Understanding Templates and Boilerplates: Templates and boilerplates serve as pre-designed frameworks that can be adapted for specific content creation needs. They typically include placeholders or guidelines that you can fill in or modify according to the specific details of your task.

Example: A template for customer service emails might include a standard greeting, space for a personalized response, and a closing line thanking the customer for their loyalty.

Benefits of Using Templates: The primary benefits of using templates include increased efficiency, consistency, and the assurance of quality. Templates help streamline the writing process by providing a clear structure to follow, which is particularly useful when dealing with high volumes of content or tight deadlines.

Example: For a series of press releases, a template ensures that all releases share a consistent format, tone, and structure, reinforcing brand identity and communication standards.

Customizing Templates for Different Tasks: While templates provide a basic structure, they are designed to be flexible and customizable. Depending on your needs, you can adjust various elements of a template to better fit the specific requirements of your project or audience.

Example: If you have a template for blog posts, you can adapt it for different topics by altering the introduction, adding relevant subheadings, and modifying the call to action at the end.

Creating Your Own Templates: If existing templates do not fully meet your needs, consider creating your own. This can be done by analyzing successful pieces of content you have produced in the past and identifying the key components that can be standardized.

Example: After writing several successful business proposals, you might create a template that includes an executive summary, problem statement, solution overview, and budget breakdown.

Sharing and Improving Templates: Templates can be shared with team members to ensure everyone produces content that meets the same standards. Additionally, feedback from users can help improve templates over time, making them more effective and user-friendly.

Example: Distribute a newsletter template to your marketing team, and periodically review it together to make suggestions for improvements based on reader feedback and evolving content strategies.

Using AI to Enhance Templates: Leverage AI tools like GPT-4 to automate parts of your templates. For instance, AI can generate data-driven content, suggest improvements, or even personalize text based on user data integrated into the template.

Example: Use GPT-4 to automatically populate sections of a financial report template with the latest market analysis and predictions based on the most recent data.

By integrating templates and boilerplates into your workflow, you not only enhance the efficiency and consistency of your content production process but also maintain a high standard of quality. Templates are adaptable, scalable, and an essential tool for anyone regularly producing varied content types.

2.6 Leveraging GPT-4's Contextual Understanding

PT-4's ability to understand context is a standout feature that significantly enhances its utility across various applications. This advanced contextual understanding allows the AI to maintain coherence over extended interactions and deliver nuanced responses. This section will guide you on how to craft prompts that fully leverage this capability, optimizing the efficiency and coherence of your interactions with GPT-4.

Understanding Contextual Understanding: GPT-4's training includes a vast array of texts, enabling it to recognize and utilize context much like a human conversational partner would. This means it can remember earlier parts of a conversation or document and apply that context to produce relevant and appropriate responses.

Example: In a dialogue about environmental policies, if you mention specific legislation early in the conversation, GPT-4 can reference or build upon that information in subsequent responses without needing repeated reminders.

Crafting Context-Rich Prompts: To take full advantage of GPT-4's contextual capabilities, your prompts should be rich in specific details that guide the AI's understanding of your expectations.

Example: Instead of asking, "What are the effects of climate change?" specify, "Discuss the effects of climate change on coastal cities, particularly focusing on sea-level rise and its impact on urban infrastructure since the 20th century."

Building on Previous Interactions: One of GPT-4's strengths is its ability to maintain context over a session. You can build progressively complex queries based on the information given in previous responses, creating a seamless and enriching interaction.

Example: Start with, "What is the current state of electric vehicle technology?" Follow up with, "How do the advancements you mentioned impact battery life and charging times?"

Sequencing Information: When dealing with complex topics, break down the information into a sequence of prompts that logically build on each other. This helps GPT-4 provide responses that are not only contextually accurate but also incrementally informative.

Example: Begin with a general overview, "Describe the basic principles of quantum computing." Then, progress to more detailed inquiries, "Explain how quantum entanglement can be used in computing to enhance processing speed."

Utilizing Contextual Cues: Explicitly include contextual cues in your prompts when you want GPT-4 to consider certain aspects or ignore others. This is particularly useful in refining the focus of the response to suit specific needs or audiences.

Example: "Write a brief for policymakers on the necessity of renewable energy, emphasizing economic benefits and referencing recent studies on job creation in the renewable sector."

Linking Prompts to Current Contexts: Integrate current events or recent data into your prompts to make the interaction more relevant and timely, thus utilizing GPT-4's ability to connect with real-world contexts.

Example: "Analyze how recent wildfires in California are related to global climate change and discuss the implications for future urban planning."

Continuous Learning and Feedback: Use feedback from the quality of responses you receive to continuously refine how you incorporate context into your prompts. This learning loop will enhance your ability to craft even more effective prompts over time.

Example: If responses to prompts about technological trends are too generic, you might add, "Provide specific examples from the last two years to illustrate each trend mentioned."

By effectively leveraging GPT-4's contextual understanding, you can enhance the depth and relevance of your interactions, making them smoother and more productive. This ability to work with context not only improves the efficiency of information retrieval and content generation but also ensures that outputs are significantly more tailored and useful.

2.7 Prompt Engineering Tools and Platforms

To maximize the potential of your interactions with GPT-4, it's beneficial to leverage various tools and platforms specifically designed to assist in creating and testing prompts. These resources can streamline the process, enhance the quality of your prompts, and provide valuable insights into how to optimize your queries. This section will introduce you to some of the best software and platforms available for prompt engineering.

Understanding Prompt Engineering Tools: Prompt engineering tools and platforms are designed to help users interact more effectively with AI models. They offer features such as prompt testing, optimization suggestions, and analytics to ensure that your prompts yield the best possible responses.

Popular Tools and Platforms:
1. OpenAI Playground:

Overview:
OpenAI Playground is a web-based interface created by OpenAI that allows users to directly interact with GPT-4. It serves as a practical tool for experimenting with different prompts and observing how changes impact the AI's responses.

Features: Users can adjust settings such as response length, style, and temperature to control the creativity level of the AI. It also allows for saving experiments, sharing them, and embedding results.

Use Case: This tool is excellent for educators, researchers, or marketers interested in exploring how AI can be applied in various scenarios.
How to Access: Visit OpenAI's official website, navigate to the Playground section, and sign in or create an account to start experimenting.

2. PromptHero:

Overview: PromptHero offers a vast collection of customizable prompt templates across multiple domains, presented on a user-friendly platform.

Features: The platform provides a curated set of effective prompt templates along with tools for easy modification and adaptation to different needs.

Use Case: Ideal for businesses looking to streamline content creation or individuals new to AI who seek structured templates.

How to Access: Go to the PromptHero website, create an account, and you can begin using and customizing templates immediately.

3. AI Dungeon:

Overview: AI Dungeon is a unique platform that uses AI to create interactive, choose-your-own-adventure stories that evolve based on user input.

Features: The platform dynamically generates content as users make narrative choices, providing a highly engaging and creative experience.

Use Case: Perfect for writers, game designers, or anyone interested in the creative potential of AI in storytelling.

How to Access: AI Dungeon is available through its website and mobile apps on the App Store and Google Play. Users need to register to start creating stories.

4.Promptor:

Overview: Designed for advanced users, Promptor offers detailed analytics and suggestions for optimizing prompt engineering.

Features: It includes performance tracking for different prompts, A/B testing capabilities, and AI-driven improvement suggestions.

Use Case: Suitable for developers, data scientists, and AI researchers focused on fine-tuning AI interactions for maximum output.

How to Access: Register on Promptor's website; some advanced features may require a subscription.

5. ChatGPT Plugins:

Overview: These browser extensions integrate GPT-4 directly into a user's browser, facilitating seamless AI interactions within any webpage.

Features: Enable real-time AI assistance for tasks like summarizing articles, generating replies, or coding help.

Use Case: Useful for professionals and students who need immediate AI assistance during online research or interaction.

How to Access: Install a ChatGPT plugin from the Chrome Web Store or equivalent browser store. Some plugins may require an API key from OpenAI.

6. GPT-3/GPT-4 API Integration:

Overview: OpenAI provides API access allowing developers to integrate GPT-4 functionalities into their own applications.

Features: Offers complete customization and automation of AI interactions, suitable for embedding within various software applications or digital products.

Use Case: Ideal for enterprises and tech teams aiming to enhance their applications with advanced AI capabilities.

How to Access: API access is available through OpenAI's platform. Users must apply for access and, once approved, can use the provided documentation to integrate the API.

Tips for Using Prompt Engineering Tools:

Experiment Regularly: Use tools like OpenAI Playground to frequently test various prompts, exploring how different phrasings affect AI responses.

Analyze and Optimize: Employ platforms like Promptor to analyze performance and refine prompts based on empirical data.

Utilize Templates: Begin with templates from services like PromptHero to save time and ensure quality starting points.

Feedback Loops: Implement feedback mechanisms from platforms like AI Dungeon to iteratively enhance prompt efficacy based on actual performance.

Integrate into Workflow: Incorporate browser plugins or APIs to embed AI capabilities directly into your daily digital tools for streamlined processes.

By leveraging these tools and platforms, you can significantly improve the effectiveness and efficiency of your interactions with GPT-4, ensuring you achieve the best results in your AI-driven projects.

Chapter 3:

Advanced Prompt Crafting Techniques

3.1 Specialized Prompts for Every Need

Advanced prompt crafting techniques can significantly enhance the effectiveness of AI tools like GPT-4 across a wide range of applications. Whether you're composing a novel, drafting a business report, or creating engaging social media content, there's a specialized prompt for that. This section will delve into various use cases across different industries, illustrating how tailored prompts can meet specific needs with precision. We'll explore how to craft these specialized prompts with examples for marketing, education, finance, social media, and blogging.

Marketing: Crafting Prompts for Persuasive Content

Overview: In marketing, prompts need to generate content that persuades and engages potential customers. This includes product descriptions, ad copy, and email marketing campaigns.

Example Prompt: "Generate a catchy, concise email subject line and body for promoting our new eco-friendly skincare line, highlighting the product's natural ingredients and environmental benefits."

Education: Enhancing Learning and Engagement

Overview: For educational purposes, prompts must be designed to facilitate learning, create interactive lesson plans, or generate educational content that is informative and engaging.

Example Prompt: "Create a detailed lesson plan for a 9th-grade biology class that introduces the concept of photosynthesis. Include a hands-on experiment that can be conducted using common household items."

Finance: Generating Data-Driven Insights

Overview: In the finance sector, prompts are often used to analyze trends, generate reports, and provide investment advice based on quantitative data.

Example Prompt: "Analyze the latest trends in the stock market for technology companies and provide an investment outlook for the next quarter based on recent performance metrics."

Social Media: Engaging a Digital Audience

Overview: Social media prompts need to generate content that is engaging, timely, and likely to encourage interaction such as likes, shares, and comments.

Example Prompt: "Create a series of tweet-sized tips about personal finance tailored for millennials, ensuring each tweet encourages engagement through questions or calls to action."

Bloggers: Creating Rich, Informative Content

Overview: Bloggers require prompts that help them produce rich, informative, and SEO-friendly content that caters to the interests and needs of their specific audience.

Example Prompt: "Draft a comprehensive guide on the best practices for organic gardening in urban environments, including a list of easy-to-grow plants and DIY container gardening tips."

Implementing Specialized Prompts: To effectively implement these specialized prompts, consider the following strategies:

Tailor to Audience: Understand who your audience is and what they are interested in to tailor your prompts accordingly.

Incorporate Specific Keywords: Use industry-specific keywords in your prompts to ensure the content is relevant and targeted.

Focus on Desired Outcomes: Be clear about what you want the AI to achieve with the response. Whether it's educating, selling, or engaging, your prompt should align with your end goal.

Iterative Refinement: Use initial responses to refine and tweak your prompts for better accuracy and engagement.

By mastering the art of crafting specialized prompts tailored to specific industries and needs, you can leverage the full potential of GPT-4 to produce highly effective, customized content. This tailored approach not only enhances the relevance and quality of the outputs but also ensures that they meet the precise needs of your target audience or business objectives.

3.2 Unleashing Creativity - Prompts for Writers

For writers, both novice and seasoned, the daunting specter of writer's block can often loom large. Fortunately, GPT-4 offers a toolkit brimming with creative potential that can help to break through these blocks and ignite the creative process. This section focuses on how writers can harness the power of GPT-4 to generate ideas, develop characters, plot out stories, and enrich their writing.

Using GPT-4 to Generate Ideas: One of the most significant advantages of using GPT-4 for writers is its ability to produce a diverse range of ideas quickly. Whether you're looking for the next big plot twist or searching for inspiration for a blog post, GPT-4 can provide a multitude of suggestions based on a few simple prompts.

Example Prompt: "Generate five unique science fiction plot ideas centered around the theme of artificial intelligence uprising."

Developing Characters and Settings: GPT-4 can assist writers in fleshing out detailed, compelling characters and immersive settings. By providing a few initial details, you can use GPT-4 to elaborate and expand these into fully realized profiles and worlds.

Example Prompt: "Create a detailed backstory for a character named Elara, a young sorceress from a deserted island, including her motivations, fears, and greatest strengths."

Plot Structuring: Structuring a plot can be a complex task, requiring the careful balancing of narrative pacing, themes, and character development. GPT-4 can help outline basic structures or suggest developments at various story points, making it easier to build a cohesive and engaging narrative.

Example Prompt: "Outline a three-act structure for a mystery novel set in Victorian London, incorporating a surprise twist involving the main detective."

Dialogue Creation: Crafting natural, dynamic dialogue is crucial for character development and story progression. GPT-4 can generate sample dialogues that can be used as a basis for refining conversations between characters.

Example Prompt: "Generate a dialogue between two rival chefs in a competitive cooking show, discussing their strategies and personal stakes in winning the competition."

Overcoming Writer's Block: When writer's block strikes, GPT-4 can be used to offer new angles and perspectives on a story, or simply to continue a narrative thread when you feel stuck.

Example Prompt: "Continue the following story from where it stops: 'As the sun set over the horizon, Lydia knew that it was now or never to confront her destiny.'"

Integrating Poetry and Experimental Writing: GPT-4 is not limited to prose; it can also be an excellent tool for poets and experimental writers looking to explore new styles or push the boundaries of conventional writing formats.

Example Prompt: "Write a poem in the style of a Shakespearean sonnet about modern-day technology."

Feedback and Refinement: In addition to generating content, GPT-4 can provide constructive feedback on written works, suggesting areas for improvement or highlighting strengths. This makes it a valuable tool for editing and refining drafts.

Example Prompt: "Review the following short story excerpt and provide feedback on character development and narrative tension."

By leveraging these techniques, writers can harness GPT-4 as a powerful ally in the creative process. Not only does it help generate fresh ideas and content, but it also assists in structuring narratives, creating rich characters, and overcoming the challenges of writer's block. Whether you're drafting the next bestselling novel or crafting compelling articles, GPT-4 can be an invaluable resource in your creative arsenal.

3.3 The Technical Writer's Ally - Generating Documentation

Technical writing encompasses a unique set of challenges, requiring precision, clarity, and often a high level of detail. GPT-4, with its advanced language capabilities, can be a vital tool for technical writers looking to streamline the creation of clear, concise, and accurate documentation. This section explores how GPT-4 can assist in various aspects of technical writing, from generating initial drafts to refining complex manuals.

Generating Initial Drafts: GPT-4 can significantly speed up the documentation process by creating first drafts. Technical writers can input specifications, data points, or outlines and have GPT-4 produce a structured draft that covers all essential information.

Example Prompt: "Create an initial draft for a user manual of a multi-functional printer, including sections on installation, daily use, troubleshooting, and maintenance."

Enhancing Clarity and Precision: Accuracy and clarity are paramount in technical documentation. GPT-4 can help refine text to ensure that it is not only technically accurate but also clear and easy to understand for its intended audience.

Example Prompt: "Revise this technical description to simplify complex jargon for an audience not familiar with technical terms. Focus on the process of setting up a virtual private network."

Consistency in Documentation: Maintaining consistency in terms, formatting, and style is crucial in technical documentation to avoid confusion. GPT-4 can assist in ensuring that all parts of a document or a series of documents are consistent with internal standards and guidelines.

Example Prompt: "Review this series of technical support articles to ensure consistency in terminology, style, and formatting according to our company's guidelines."

Automating Routine Writing Tasks: Many aspects of technical documentation are repetitive. GPT-4 can automate routine writing tasks such as generating standard descriptions, warning messages, or regular maintenance instructions.

Example Prompt: "Generate a standard safety warning to be included in all technical manuals for electrical kitchen appliances."

Multilingual Documentation: For global products, technical documentation often needs to be available in multiple languages. GPT-4 can assist in translating technical documents accurately and swiftly, maintaining the original's precision in various languages.

Example Prompt: "Translate the following installation instructions from English into Spanish, ensuring technical accuracy and adherence to technical terminology."

Creating Interactive Help Tools: GPT-4 can be used to create interactive help tools, such as chatbots or help sections within apps, that use the technical documentation to answer user queries in real-time.

Example Prompt: "Develop a script for a chatbot that helps users troubleshoot common issues with our software, based on our existing technical FAQ documentation."

Feedback and Continuous Improvement: GPT-4 can analyze user feedback on technical documents to suggest improvements or areas that frequently confuse readers, helping technical writers prioritize revisions.

Example Prompt: "Analyze customer feedback on our recent hardware setup guide and suggest changes to improve clarity and reduce setup time."

By integrating GPT-4 into the technical writing process, writers can not only enhance their productivity and efficiency but also improve the quality of the documentation they produce. Whether it's creating initial drafts, ensuring consistency, or translating documents, GPT-4 proves to be an invaluable ally, helping to meet the rigorous demands of technical communication.

3.4 Code Generation - A Programmer's Guide

For programmers, the ability to quickly generate and debug code can significantly accelerate development cycles and improve productivity. GPT-4 offers a powerful toolset for coding tasks, capable of writing snippets, debugging, and even explaining complex algorithms. This section will explore how to effectively use GPT-4 for code generation, providing practical examples and tips without delving into actual code responses.

Generating Code Snippets: GPT-4 can assist in generating code snippets for a variety of programming languages and frameworks. By specifying the functionality you need, GPT-4 can provide a concise, functional snippet that fits into your larger project.

Example Prompt: "Generate a Python function that takes a list of integers and returns a new list with each element squared."

Debugging Assistance: Debugging can be a time-consuming process. GPT-4 can help identify errors in your code and suggest corrections. Describe the issue you're encountering, along with any error messages, and GPT-4 can analyze the problem and offer solutions.

Example Prompt: "I'm getting a 'null pointer exception' when trying to run my Java app. Here's the function where the error occurs. What could be causing this?"

Code Optimization: Optimizing code for efficiency and performance is another area where GPT-4 can provide assistance. You can ask GPT-4 for recommendations on how to make your code cleaner and more efficient.

Example Prompt: "Review this SQL query for retrieving all transactions in the last 24 hours and suggest optimizations for improving query performance."

Algorithm Explanation and Implementation: Sometimes, understanding and implementing algorithms can be challenging. GPT-4 can explain algorithms in plain language and show how to implement them in the code, which is especially useful for learning or teaching purposes.

Example Prompt: "Explain the quicksort algorithm and how it can be implemented in C++."

Automating Routine Tasks: Many coding tasks are repetitive and can be automated. GPT-4 can help write scripts for these tasks, saving valuable time that can be better spent on more complex problems.

Example Prompt: "Write a script that automatically backs up SQL database changes every hour."

Writing Documentation: Good documentation is crucial for maintaining and scaling software projects. GPT-4 can assist in generating comprehensive documentation for your code, ensuring that future developers (or 'future you') can easily understand and work with your codebase.

Example Prompt: "Generate documentation for the following JavaScript function, including a description, parameters, return value, and a simple usage example."

Learning New Technologies: As technology evolves, staying updated with the latest programming languages and tools is essential. GPT-4 can be a resource for learning new technologies by providing explanations, examples, and best practices.

Example Prompt: "I'm new to React. Can you explain the concept of state and props and provide a simple example?"

By leveraging GPT-4, programmers can enhance their coding efficiency, improve the quality of their code, and spend more time on creative problem-solving. Whether it's generating code, debugging, optimizing, or learning new technologies, GPT-4 is an invaluable tool in any programmer's toolkit. This guide not only helps in understanding how to interact with GPT-4 for coding purposes but also ensures that these interactions lead to productive outcomes, propelling your programming projects forward.

3.5 Analyzing Data with Precision

In a world dominated by data, the ability to efficiently analyze and interpret large datasets is invaluable. GPT-4 can be a powerful ally in this realm, aiding not just in crunching numbers but in making sense of them in a way that informs decision-making and insight generation. This section will guide you on how to craft prompts that leverage GPT-4's capabilities for precise data analysis and interpretation.

Defining Clear Objectives: The first step in using GPT-4 for data analysis is to clearly define what you aim to achieve with your data. Whether it's identifying trends, predicting outcomes, or finding relationships between variables, your prompt should specify your analysis goals explicitly.

Example Prompt: "Analyze the sales data from the last quarter and identify which products are performing above expectations and which are underperforming."

Providing Data Context: To enable GPT-4 to provide relevant and accurate analyses, it's crucial to give it as much context about the data as possible. This includes not only the raw data but also any relevant background information that might affect its interpretation, such as seasonal effects, market conditions, or changes in business operations.

Example Prompt: "Given the attached customer satisfaction survey data, determine key factors that influence customer loyalty during the COVID-19 pandemic, considering changes in consumer behavior and market conditions."

Asking for Specific Analyses: GPT-4 can perform a range of statistical analyses and provide summaries that can guide more detailed exploration. When crafting your prompt, specify the type of analysis you need, such as descriptive statistics, regression analysis, or predictive modeling.

Example Prompt: "Perform a regression analysis on the attached dataset to evaluate how age, income, and education level predict online shopping behavior."

Interpreting Results: Beyond just crunching numbers, GPT-4 can help interpret the results of data analysis, explaining the implications in clear, easy-to-understand language. This is particularly valuable for sharing findings with stakeholders who may not have a technical background.

Example Prompt: "Interpret the results of the logistic regression analysis from the previous prompt and explain what the coefficients suggest about the impact of each predictor on the likelihood of making an online purchase."

Generating Visual Data Representations: Visuals can often convey insights more effectively than numbers alone. GPT-4 can assist in generating descriptions of visuals that should be created from data analysis, aiding in the communication of findings.

Example Prompt: "Suggest the most effective types of visualizations for representing the time series analysis of our monthly sales data and explain why each type is appropriate."

Ensuring Accuracy and Reliability: When dealing with critical data analysis tasks, it's important to ensure the accuracy and reliability of the outputs provided by GPT-4. This may involve cross-verifying AI-generated insights with other data sources or statistical tools.

Example Prompt: "Verify the accuracy of the AI-generated sales forecast by comparing it with historical sales trends and identify any discrepancies."

Iterative Analysis: Data analysis is often an iterative process where initial findings lead to new questions and deeper investigations. Encourage ongoing analysis by refining your prompts based on earlier insights provided by GPT-4.

Example Prompt: "Based on the previous analysis of sales trends, drill down into the underperforming product categories and analyze if specific regions or customer segments are contributing to the decline."

By mastering these techniques, you can harness GPT-4's powerful computational abilities to perform robust data analysis. Crafting precise prompts that guide the AI in processing and interpreting data not only saves time but also enhances the depth and breadth of analytical insights, driving smarter business decisions and innovative solutions

3.6 The Art of Iteration: Refining Your Prompts

Iteration is a fundamental aspect of any creative or analytical process, including working with advanced AI like GPT-4. Iterative refinement of prompts is essential for honing their effectiveness and achieving the desired output quality. This approach involves a systematic process of trial and error, where each iteration improves upon the last based on feedback and results. This section will explore strategies for refining your prompts through iterative practices, enhancing both the precision of the AI's responses and your proficiency in prompt engineering.

Starting with Broad Concepts: Begin the iterative process by crafting prompts that address broad aspects of your query or task. This initial step helps establish a baseline understanding and sets the direction for more specific inquiries.

Example Prompt: "Describe the general trends in consumer behavior regarding online shopping."

Narrowing Down Focus: Based on the initial responses, start narrowing down the focus of your prompts to target specific areas of interest or ambiguity. This step helps to deepen the exploration and clarify details that are crucial for your analysis or content creation.

Example Prompt: "Focus on the recent shift in consumer behavior towards sustainable products in online shopping."

Incorporating Feedback: Use the AI's responses as feedback for refining your prompts. Identify areas where the response may have been too vague, off-topic, or incorrect, and adjust your prompts accordingly to guide the AI more effectively.

Example Prompt: "Specify the factors influencing the surge in purchases of sustainable products online during the last quarter."

Testing Different Variations: Don't hesitate to experiment with different variations of your prompt to see which yields the best responses. Altering the wording, structure, or detail level can significantly impact the AI's output.

Example Prompt Variations: "What are the leading reasons consumers cite for choosing sustainable products?" versus "Analyze consumer reviews to identify common themes about why customers prefer sustainable products."

Utilizing Qualitative Insights: Sometimes, qualitative insights from the AI's responses can provide unexpected directions for further exploration. Be open to following these new paths and refining your prompts to incorporate these insights.

Example Prompt: "Explore how social media influences consumer perceptions of sustainability in products."

Refining Through Specificity: As you refine your prompts, aim to be as specific as possible regarding the information you need. Specificity helps reduce ambiguity and directs the AI to focus its computational resources more effectively.

Example Prompt: "Provide a detailed comparison of consumer satisfaction between sustainable products and conventional products based on customer review data from the last year."

Iterative Learning: View each interaction with GPT-4 as a learning opportunity. Over time, you'll gain insights into how different types of prompts perform and how subtle changes can affect the outcomes. This knowledge is invaluable for mastering prompt engineering.

Example Prompt Evolution: Start with broad inquiries and gradually incorporate specific elements based on previous responses to sculpt the most effective prompts.

Documentation of Changes: Keep a record of the changes you make to your prompts and the corresponding outcomes. This documentation can be crucial for understanding what works, what doesn't, and how best to approach similar tasks in the future.

Example Documentation: Maintain a log or a digital notebook detailing each version of your prompt and the quality of the response it elicited.

By embracing the art of iteration in refining your prompts, you can significantly enhance the effectiveness of your interactions with GPT-4. This process not only improves the quality of the AI-generated content but also sharpens your skills in prompt crafting, leading to more efficient and successful AI engagements over time.

3.7 Ethical Considerations in the Age of AI

As AI technologies like GPT-4 become increasingly integrated into various aspects of society, ethical considerations are paramount to ensure these tools are used responsibly. This section addresses the ethical dimensions of using GPT-4, focusing on how to employ this powerful AI in a manner that upholds standards of fairness, privacy, and accountability. We'll explore guidelines for responsible AI usage, potential ethical pitfalls, and strategies for mitigating risks.

Understanding AI Ethics: AI ethics involves a set of principles and practices aimed at ensuring the development and use of AI technologies benefit society while minimizing harm. These principles often include fairness, accountability, transparency, and respect for user privacy.

Fairness and Bias Mitigation: One of the critical ethical challenges in AI deployment is the potential for algorithmic biases that can perpetuate discrimination or unfair treatment. When using GPT-4:

Example Action: Regularly audit AI-generated content for biases. For instance, if GPT-4 is used for HR purposes, like screening resumes, it's crucial to ensure the algorithm does not favor certain demographics over others.

Guideline: Implement and adhere to fairness protocols, such as reviewing and adjusting training data and prompt structures to avoid discriminatory outcomes.

Transparency and Accountability: Users should understand how AI decisions are made, especially when these decisions affect them directly. Transparency in AI fosters trust and accountability.

Example Action: If GPT-4 is used to generate financial advice, users should be clearly informed about how conclusions are derived and the limitations of AI-generated advice.

Guideline: Develop clear documentation and communication strategies that explain the AI's role and the basis for its outputs.

Respecting Privacy: Protecting user data and respecting privacy are fundamental. GPT-4, which can process vast amounts of data, including personal information, must be managed carefully to prevent unauthorized data exposure.

Example Action: Ensure that data fed into GPT-4 for processing is anonymized where possible, or that explicit consent has been obtained for its use.

Guideline: Adhere to strict data handling and privacy policies compliant with regulations like GDPR and CCPA.

Avoiding Misuse: There is a potential for misuse of AI technologies, such as creating misleading information or impersonating individuals. Setting boundaries on how GPT-4 can be used is essential for ethical compliance.

Example Action: Implement restrictions that prevent the use of GPT-4 for creating deepfake content or other deceptive materials.

Guideline: Establish clear ethical guidelines and use cases for AI deployment within your organization.

Engaging with Stakeholders: Involving a broad range of stakeholders in discussions about how AI is used can help address diverse concerns and values, leading to more ethically robust AI applications.

Example Action: Conduct workshops or forums with users, ethicists, legal experts, and community leaders to gather input on how GPT-4 should be deployed.

Guideline: Create multi-stakeholder committees to oversee AI projects and ensure ongoing ethical reviews and adjustments.

Continuous Ethical Education: As AI evolves, so too should our understanding and approaches to ethical challenges. Continuous learning and adaptation are necessary.

Example Action: Keep abreast of the latest AI ethics research and case studies to inform the responsible development and use of GPT-4.

Guideline: Provide regular training and updates for teams working with AI to ensure they understand and can implement best ethical practices.

By embracing these ethical considerations, users of GPT-4 can help steer the development and application of AI technologies towards outcomes that are not only effective but also just and beneficial for all sections of society. This proactive approach to AI ethics is crucial to building trust and maximizing the positive impact of AI in our lives.

3.8 Utilizing GPT-4's Expanded Knowledge Base

G PT-4 is equipped with a vast and diverse knowledge base, encompassing a wide range of topics and fields. This expanded knowledge allows it to provide comprehensive responses, making it an invaluable tool for research, education, content creation, and more. However, while GPT-4 can now access live data, it is important to remember that it is still a machine. The accuracy of its responses depends on the reliability of the sources it retrieves information from. This section will guide you on how to effectively tap into GPT-4's knowledge base and ensure the quality of the information you receive.

Accessing Comprehensive Information: GPT-4's broad training allows it to cover an extensive array of subjects. When crafting prompts, you can leverage this to gain detailed and well-rounded insights.

Example Prompt: "Provide a detailed overview of the history of artificial intelligence, highlighting key milestones and influential figures."

Specifying Reliable Sources: To ensure the accuracy of the information provided, specify the type of sources or references you want GPT-4 to consider. This can help filter out unreliable information and focus on credible data.

Example Prompt: "Summarize the latest advancements in renewable energy technology, referencing articles from reputable scientific journals published in the last year."

Cross-Referencing Information: Given the potential for inaccuracies, it's wise to cross-reference the information provided by GPT-4 with other trusted sources. This step can validate the data and ensure its reliability.

Example Prompt: "Compare the economic impact of the 2008 financial crisis with the COVID-19 pandemic, using data from authoritative economic reports."

Utilizing Live Data Access: GPT-4's ability to access live data means it can provide up-to-date information on current events and trends. When using this feature, make sure to clarify the context and timeframe for the information you need.

Example Prompt: "Provide the latest statistics on global vaccination rates for COVID-19 as of this month, including sources from major health organizations like the WHO and CDC."

Deep Dives into Specialized Topics: For more niche or specialized topics, GPT-4 can offer in-depth explanations and analyses. Clearly state your area of interest and any specific angles you wish to explore.

Example Prompt: "Explain the principles and applications of quantum computing in layman's terms, and discuss its potential impact on cybersecurity."

Ensuring Contextual Relevance: When seeking comprehensive responses, it's crucial to provide enough context to guide the AI. This helps GPT-4 tailor its responses to your specific needs and ensures the information is relevant and focused.

Example Prompt: "Analyze the role of social media in political campaigns over the past decade, with a focus on its impact on voter engagement and opinion formation."

Using Detailed Queries for Complex Analyses: For complex analyses, break down your queries into detailed, manageable parts. This method helps in obtaining thorough and accurate responses by guiding the AI through each aspect of the topic.

Example Prompt: "Discuss the causes and consequences of climate change, including the scientific consensus, major contributing factors, and the socio-economic impacts on vulnerable populations."

Fact-Checking and Validation: After receiving responses from GPT-4, particularly for critical or sensitive information, conduct additional fact-checking and validation to ensure the data's integrity.

Example Prompt: "Draft a report on the effects of artificial intelligence on job markets, using data from recent studies and reports. Verify the key findings with current labor market statistics."

Engaging with Updated Information: Given GPT-4's capability to access real-time data, use it to stay informed about the latest developments in fast-changing fields like technology, medicine, and finance.

Example Prompt: "What are the latest trends in blockchain technology and cryptocurrency regulation? Include information from the past six months."

By effectively utilizing GPT-4's expanded knowledge base and incorporating these strategies, you can tap into a wealth of information to generate comprehensive and reliable content. Always be mindful of the need for validation and cross-referencing to maintain the accuracy and credibility of the data you use. This balanced approach will help you maximize the benefits of GPT-4's capabilities while ensuring the integrity of your outputs.

3.9 Multi-turn Prompt Strategies

Engaging in longer, more complex conversations with GPT-4 requires a strategic approach to maintain coherence and relevance over multiple interactions. Multi-turn prompts are essential for tasks that involve detailed exploration, iterative questioning, or ongoing dialogues. This section will guide you on how to effectively manage and craft multi-turn prompt strategies to ensure your conversations with GPT-4 remain focused and productive.

Establishing Context Early: Begin by clearly setting the context for the conversation. This helps GPT-4 understand the background and objectives from the outset, which is crucial for maintaining relevance throughout the interaction.

Example Prompt: "I need to understand the impacts of climate change on coastal cities. Let's start with an overview of the primary effects of climate change on sea levels."

Building Sequentially: Structure your prompts to build on the information provided in previous responses. This approach helps create a logical flow and ensures that each turn of the conversation adds depth to the discussion.

Example Prompt Sequence:
Initial: "Explain how rising sea levels affect coastal infrastructure."

Follow-up: "What are the long-term economic impacts of these effects on coastal communities?"

Referencing Previous Responses: To maintain coherence, reference key points from previous responses in your new prompts. This technique reinforces continuity and helps the AI keep track of the conversation's progress.

Example Prompt: "Based on your earlier explanation of the economic impacts, how might these changes influence migration patterns in affected regions?"

Clarifying and Redirecting: If the AI's response goes off track or lacks clarity, use your next prompt to clarify your needs or redirect the conversation. This helps ensure that the dialogue remains aligned with your goals.

Example Prompt: "You mentioned migration patterns. Can you elaborate on how environmental changes specifically drive migration from rural to urban areas?"

Incorporating Feedback: Use feedback loops to refine your prompts based on the responses you receive. Ask for clarifications or more details as needed to deepen the exploration.

Example Prompt: "You provided an overview of urban migration. Can you give specific examples of cities that have experienced significant population changes due to climate-related factors?"

Handling Complex Topics: For intricate subjects, break down the conversation into smaller, manageable segments. Address one aspect at a time to avoid overwhelming the AI and to keep the discussion focused.

Example Prompt Sequence:
Initial: "Describe the role of renewable energy in mitigating climate change."
Follow-up: "How has the adoption of solar energy specifically impacted carbon emissions in the past decade?"

Summarizing and Recapping: Periodically summarize the information covered to reinforce understanding and provide a clear transition to the next topic or question. This practice helps maintain coherence and clarity.

Example Prompt: "To summarize, we've discussed the economic and migratory impacts of climate change. Now, let's explore the policy measures that have been effective in addressing these challenges."

Managing Longer Interactions: For extended conversations, it's helpful to periodically reset the context and remind the AI of the ongoing objectives. This helps the AI maintain focus over multiple interactions.

Example Prompt: "We've covered several aspects of climate change impacts. Let's shift to discussing potential future scenarios and predictions based on current data."

Utilizing Multi-turn Strategies in Specific Scenarios: Different scenarios may require tailored multi-turn strategies. For instance, in technical troubleshooting, step-by-step guidance ensures clarity and resolution.

Example Prompt Sequence for Troubleshooting:

Initial: "I'm having trouble with my Python script. It's throwing a syntax error. Can you help identify the issue?"

Follow-up: "Here's the error message I received. What steps should I take to resolve it?"

By implementing these multi-turn prompt strategies, you can effectively manage longer conversations with GPT-4, ensuring that they remain coherent, relevant, and productive. This structured approach not only enhances the quality of the interaction but also maximizes the depth and value of the information obtained from the AI.

3.10 Using AI for Multilingual Tasks

In our increasingly globalized world, the ability to communicate and create content across different languages and cultural contexts is crucial. GPT-4, with its expansive training data, is well-equipped to handle tasks in multiple languages, offering opportunities for broadening outreach and understanding diverse audiences. This section focuses on how to effectively create prompts that utilize GPT-4's capabilities for multilingual tasks, ensuring accurate and culturally relevant outputs.

Understanding Multilingual Capabilities: GPT-4 supports numerous languages, enabling you to engage with global audiences in their native languages. Start by familiarizing yourself with the AI's language capabilities to ensure that your prompts are aligned with what the AI can effectively handle.

Example Prompt: "List all the languages you can generate content in and identify which ones you can support with advanced capabilities such as technical writing or poetry."

Crafting Language-Specific Prompts: When creating prompts in different languages, consider linguistic nuances and cultural relevance. Tailor your prompts to reflect the language structure and cultural context to enhance the quality and appropriateness of the AI-generated content.

Example Prompt: "Write a short introduction about renewable energy benefits in Japanese, considering Japan's specific energy policies and cultural attitudes towards environmental conservation."

Ensuring Cultural Relevance: Beyond translation, cultural relevance is crucial in creating content that resonates with a particular audience. Research cultural preferences, norms, and current trends in the target region to inform the way you structure your prompts.

Example Prompt: "Create a marketing brochure for a new fitness app, styled for a Brazilian audience, emphasizing community and family aspects which are significant in Brazilian culture."

Using Bilingual Prompts: To ensure accuracy in content generation, use bilingual prompts where necessary. This can help the AI understand the context better, especially when dealing with complex topics or less common languages.

Example Prompt: "Explain the concept of sustainable investing in both English and Arabic, focusing on the importance of this practice in Middle Eastern financial markets."

Feedback and Iteration in Multiple Languages: Utilize feedback from native speakers to refine and iterate on the AI-generated content. This feedback is invaluable for improving accuracy and cultural appropriateness.

Example Prompt: "Review the French text on culinary traditions of Provence and suggest changes to enhance authenticity and appeal to local gastronomy enthusiasts."

Cross-Cultural Adaptations: When adapting content across cultures, consider how different elements need to be modified to meet local expectations and regulations. This might include changing examples, idioms, and even the tone of the message.

Example Prompt: "Adapt this public health advisory on sunscreen use from Australian English to Arabic, considering the Middle Eastern climate and cultural practices regarding sun exposure."

Handling Multilingual Customer Support: In customer support scenarios, prompts can be designed to handle inquiries in multiple languages, streamlining operations and improving user satisfaction.

Example Prompt: "Generate a response to a customer complaint in Spanish, ensuring politeness and offering a solution based on our refund policy."

Legal and Ethical Considerations: When operating across languages, be mindful of legal and ethical standards in different regions, especially regarding data privacy, consumer rights, and content regulation.

Example Prompt: "Draft a privacy policy notice for an online store in both German and English, compliant with GDPR and local German data protection laws."

By strategically using GPT-4 for multilingual tasks, you can effectively bridge language barriers and enhance global communication. This approach not only broadens your reach but also deepens engagement by producing content that is linguistically accurate and culturally attuned. With thoughtful prompt engineering and an understanding of cultural nuances, GPT-4 can serve as a powerful tool in your multilingual communication strategy.

Chapter 4:

Putting It All Into Practice

4.1 Case Studies: Real-World Success Stories

GPT-4 has been successfully utilized across a wide range of industries, proving its versatility and power in enhancing creative processes, optimizing workflows, and delivering tailored customer experiences. This section explores real-world applications of GPT-4 in various fields, illustrating how businesses and individuals alike have harnessed this technology to achieve remarkable outcomes.

Content Creation: Businesses leverage GPT-4 to generate engaging content efficiently, from product descriptions to comprehensive blog posts. By using AI to craft content, companies ensure consistency and quality while saving significant time and resources.

Case Study: A leading e-commerce platform uses GPT-4 to create detailed product descriptions that are not only informative but also SEO-optimized. This approach has led to improved search engine rankings and an increase in organic traffic.

Search Engine Optimization (SEO): Crafting website content optimized for search engines is crucial for digital visibility. GPT-4 assists in generating content that naturally incorporates targeted keywords, enhancing search rankings and driving more organic traffic.

Case Study: A digital marketing agency uses GPT-4 to develop SEO-friendly articles for clients in various niches. By optimizing content around specific keywords, the agency has seen a significant boost in clients' search engine performance and user engagement.

Marketing & Advertising: AI-driven prompts are employed to personalize marketing efforts, from email campaigns to social media ads, ensuring that messages resonate with the intended audience and lead to higher conversion rates.

Case Study: A fashion retail company uses GPT-4 to craft personalized email marketing campaigns that suggest products based on previous purchasing behavior, resulting in a 25% increase in conversion rates.

Creative Exploration: Writers and artists use GPT-4 to break through creative blocks and explore new ideas. Whether for writing, art, or design, AI prompts provide a springboard for creativity, offering fresh perspectives and unexpected concepts.

Case Study: An author struggling with writer's block uses GPT-4 to generate plot ideas and character dialogues, which helps to complete a novel that was stalled for months.

Education & Training: Educators utilize GPT-4 to create customized learning materials that adapt to different learning styles, making education more accessible and engaging for students of all ages.

Case Study: A language learning app integrates GPT-4 to offer personalized practice exercises and conversational interactions, enhancing user experience and learning outcomes.

Customer Service Chatbots: AI-driven chatbots powered by GPT-4 handle customer inquiries and resolve issues efficiently, ensuring 24/7 customer service support and freeing human agents to tackle more complex problems.

Case Study: A telecommunications company implements a GPT-4 powered chatbot to handle basic customer service inquiries, reducing response times and improving customer satisfaction ratings.

Code Generation: Programmers use GPT-4 to generate code snippets or even complete functionalities, accelerating development cycles and reducing human error.

Case Study: A software development startup uses GPT-4 to generate and debug code, cutting down development time by 30% and significantly reducing bugs in the initial software releases.

Data Analysis & Research: Researchers employ GPT-4 to sift through large datasets, generate insights, and even draft research papers, streamlining the scientific discovery process.

Case Study: A pharmaceutical company uses GPT-4 to analyze clinical trial data, identifying potential adverse effects more quickly and accelerating the path to drug approval.

Product Design & Development: GPT-4 aids in the early stages of product design by generating ideas and prototypes based on specific user needs, thus speeding up the design process and introducing innovative solutions.

Case Study: An automotive company uses GPT-4 to brainstorm and prototype new vehicle safety features, leading to groundbreaking innovations in their latest models.

Art & Music Generation: Artists and musicians use GPT-4 to create unique works of art and compositions, exploring new realms of creativity and collaborative art forms.

Case Study: A composer collaborates with GPT-4 to create a symphony where each movement is inspired by different historical eras, resulting in a critically acclaimed piece that blends classical influences with modern computational creativity.

These case studies demonstrate the diverse applications of GPT-4 across sectors, highlighting its role in driving innovation, improving efficiency, and enhancing creative processes. By integrating AI into various aspects of work and creativity, industries are not only able to achieve more with less but are also pushing the boundaries of what's possible in their fields.

4.2 Community Wisdom: Learning from Others

The power of GPT-4 is amplified when we share knowledge and learn from each other's experiences. Joining the community of GPT-4 users opens up a wealth of collective wisdom, providing insights, tips, and tricks that can enhance your use of this powerful AI. This section explores the benefits of engaging with the GPT-4 community, highlights how to leverage shared experiences, and encourages you to contribute your own discoveries.

Engaging with Online Forums: Online forums dedicated to GPT-4 and AI discussions are rich resources for learning. These platforms allow users to ask questions, share experiences, and provide solutions to common challenges.

Example: Joining forums like Reddit's r/OpenAI or AI-specific subreddits can connect you with a diverse group of users who share their practical tips on optimizing prompts, troubleshooting issues, and innovative use cases.

Participating in Webinars and Workshops: Many organizations and community groups offer webinars and workshops focused on using GPT-4 effectively. These sessions often feature experts who provide deep dives into specific aspects of the AI and share advanced techniques.

Example: Attending webinars hosted by AI conferences or educational institutions can provide you with up-to-date knowledge on the latest advancements in GPT-4 and practical applications across different fields.

Sharing and Learning through Social Media: Social media platforms, particularly LinkedIn, Twitter, and specialized AI communities, are great places to follow industry leaders, join discussions, and stay informed about the latest trends and innovations in AI.

Example: Following hashtags like #GPT4 or #AIPromptEngineering on Twitter can lead you to valuable threads where professionals share their latest experiments and findings.

Collaborating on GitHub and Code Repositories: GitHub and other code-sharing platforms host numerous projects and repositories where developers collaborate on GPT-4 applications. These repositories often include detailed documentation and examples that can be incredibly educational.

Example: Contributing to or using repositories such as OpenAI's official GitHub page or other community-driven projects can provide you with practical examples and collaborative opportunities.

Attending AI Meetups and Conferences: In-person or virtual meetups and conferences are excellent opportunities to network with other GPT-4 users, learn from expert presentations, and participate in hands-on workshops.

Example: Joining local AI meetups or attending conferences like AI Expo or OpenAI Summits can enhance your understanding and provide networking opportunities with fellow enthusiasts and professionals.

Reading Blogs and Case Studies: Many AI practitioners and organizations maintain blogs where they share in-depth case studies, tutorials, and insights on using GPT-4. These resources can offer valuable lessons from real-world applications.

Example: Following blogs from AI researchers or companies like OpenAI, AI Dungeon, or independent experts can keep you updated with new techniques and success stories.

Contributing Your Knowledge: Sharing your own experiences and tips with the community not only helps others but also solidifies your own understanding and positions you as a knowledgeable member of the community.

Example: Writing articles or blog posts about your unique use cases, challenges you've overcome, and tips for optimizing GPT-4 can contribute significantly to the collective knowledge base.

Joining Professional Networks: Professional networks and associations for AI professionals often have resources, forums, and events specifically designed for skill development and knowledge sharing.

Example: Joining organizations like the Association for the Advancement of Artificial Intelligence (AAAI) or participating in specialized AI groups on platforms like LinkedIn can connect you with experts and peers in the field.

Learning from Open Source Projects: Many open source projects use GPT-4 and provide detailed explanations of their implementation and usage, offering a treasure trove of learning material.

Example: Exploring open source projects on platforms like GitHub that utilize GPT-4 can help you understand practical applications and inspire your own projects.

By engaging with the GPT-4 community, you can tap into a vast pool of shared wisdom, enhancing your ability to use this technology effectively. The collective experiences and insights of fellow users can provide valuable shortcuts to learning and open new possibilities for creative and professional applications. Embrace the opportunity to learn from others and contribute your own knowledge, making the most of the collaborative spirit that drives the AI community.

4.3 Step-by-Step Exercises to Practice Prompt Crafting Skills

Hands-on practice is the most effective way to master the art of prompt crafting. By engaging in practical exercises, you can build and refine your skills, making your interactions with GPT-4 more efficient and productive. This section provides a series of step-by-step exercises designed to help you hone your prompt crafting abilities.

Exercise 1: Basic Prompt Structure

Objective: Learn to create clear and concise prompts.
Instructions:
1. Start with a simple task, such as generating a summary of a news article.
2. Write a basic prompt: "Summarize the key points of the latest news article on climate change."
3. Review the AI's response and adjust the prompt for clarity and specificity.
4. Refine your prompt to include more details: "Summarize the key points of the latest news article on climate change, focusing on its impact on polar ice caps."

Exercise 2: Using Context Effectively

Objective: Practice providing context to improve response relevance.
Instructions:
1. Choose a topic, such as renewable energy.
2. Write a prompt that includes context: "Explain the benefits of solar energy for residential use."
3. Add more context to refine the response: "Explain the benefits of solar energy for residential use, considering cost savings, environmental impact, and government incentives."
4. Compare the responses and note how added context enhances the quality.

Exercise 3: Crafting Multi-Turn Prompts

Objective: Develop skills in maintaining coherence over multiple interactions.
Instructions:
1. Begin with a broad question: "What are the causes of deforestation?"
2. Based on the AI's response, ask a follow-up question: "How does deforestation affect biodiversity?"
3. Continue the conversation: "What measures can be taken to combat deforestation?"
4. Evaluate the coherence and depth of the conversation and refine prompts as needed.

Exercise 4: Using Specific Instructions and Keywords

Objective: Learn to use keywords and specific instructions to guide the AI.
Instructions:
1. Select a task, such as writing a product description.
2. Write a prompt using specific instructions: "Write a product description for a new smartphone, highlighting its camera quality, battery life, and innovative features."

3. Include keywords to focus the response: "Write a product description for a new 5G smartphone, highlighting its 48MP camera, 5000mAh battery, and AI-based features."

4. Review and refine based on the AI's output.

Exercise 5: Refining Prompts Through Iteration

Objective: Practice iterative refinement to improve prompt outcomes.
Instructions:

1. Start with a general prompt: "Describe the history of artificial intelligence."

2. Analyze the response and identify areas for improvement.

3. Refine the prompt: "Describe the history of artificial intelligence, focusing on key developments from the 1950s to the present."

4. Continue to iterate: "Describe the history of artificial intelligence, focusing on key developments from the 1950s to the present, and highlight significant breakthroughs and their impact on modern technology."

Exercise 6: Enhancing Creativity with Prompts

Objective: Use prompts to stimulate creative writing and idea generation.
Instructions:
1. Choose a creative task, such as writing a short story.

2. Write an open-ended prompt: "Write a short story about a time traveler who visits ancient Rome."

3. Add creative elements to guide the story: "Write a short story about a time traveler who visits ancient Rome and gets involved in a political conspiracy."

4. Experiment with different prompts to see how they influence the narrative direction and creativity.

Exercise 7: Combining Multiple Techniques

Objective: Integrate various prompt crafting techniques to achieve complex tasks.

Instructions:

1. Define a complex task, such as creating a marketing campaign.

2. Start with a broad prompt: "Develop a marketing campaign for a new electric vehicle."

3. Add context and specific instructions: "Develop a marketing campaign for a new electric vehicle, targeting environmentally conscious consumers, and highlight its zero-emission technology and cost-saving benefits."

4. Use multi-turn prompts to build the campaign: "What social media strategies should be included in the campaign?" Followed by, "How can we measure the effectiveness of the campaign?"

Exercise 8: Simulating Customer Interactions

Objective: Use AI to simulate customer service scenarios.

Instructions:

1. Write a prompt to simulate a customer inquiry: "How can I return a product I bought online?"

2. Follow up with clarifying questions based on the response: "What is the return policy for electronics purchased online?"

3. Develop responses to common follow-up questions: "What are the steps for processing a return?"

Exercise 9: Translating and Adapting Content

Objective: Practice using AI for multilingual tasks.

Instructions:

1. Write a prompt for translation: "Translate the following product description into Spanish."

2. Add context for cultural adaptation: "Translate the following product description into Spanish, ensuring it appeals to a Latin American audience."

3. Review the translation for accuracy and cultural relevance.

Exercise 10: Generating Technical Documentation

Objective: Use AI to create technical documentation.
Instructions:

1. Write a prompt to generate a user manual: "Create a user manual for a new smart thermostat, including installation instructions and troubleshooting tips."

2. Add detailed sections: "Expand the manual to include a FAQ section addressing common issues users might face."

3. Refine the content for clarity and technical accuracy.

Exercise 11: Developing Educational Content

Objective: Craft prompts to generate educational materials.
Instructions:

1. Write a prompt for lesson plans: "Develop a lesson plan for a high school biology class on the topic of cell division."

2. Include interactive elements: "Include hands-on activities and experiments to help students understand mitosis and meiosis."

3. Review and adjust based on the educational level and engagement.

Exercise 12: Creating Marketing Copy
Objective: Use AI to generate compelling marketing copy.
Instructions:

1. Write a prompt for an advertisement: "Write an advertisement for a new eco-friendly water bottle."

2. Focus on unique selling points: "Highlight the water bottle's sustainability features and health benefits."

3. Refine the copy to ensure it is persuasive and engaging.

Exercise 13: Analyzing Market Trends

Objective: Use AI to analyze and interpret market data.

Instructions:

1. Write a prompt to analyze trends: "Analyze recent market trends in the technology sector."

2. Focus on specific areas: "Identify key drivers of growth in the smartphone market."

3. Refine the analysis to provide actionable insights.

Exercise 14: Conducting Interviews

Objective: Use AI to simulate interview scenarios.

Instructions:

1. Write a prompt to simulate a job interview: "Conduct a job interview for a software developer position."

2. Follow up with detailed questions: "What is your experience with agile development methodologies?"

3.Review the responses and refine the questions for clarity and relevance.

Exercise 15: Writing Reviews and Summaries

Objective: Craft prompts to generate reviews and summaries.

Instructions:

1. Write a prompt for a book review: "Write a review of the book 'To Kill a Mockingbird'."

2. Include specific elements: "Discuss the themes, character development, and overall impact of the book."

3. Refine the review for depth and coherence.

Exercise 16: Developing Product Recommendations

Objective: Use AI to generate personalized product recommendations.
Instructions:

1. Write a prompt for recommendations: "Recommend products for a customer looking for eco-friendly household items."

2. Include customer preferences: "Focus on products that are sustainable, affordable, and highly rated."

3. Refine the recommendations based on user feedback.

Exercise 17: Enhancing Social Media Engagement

Objective: Use AI to create engaging social media content.
Instructions:

1. Write a prompt for social media posts: "Create a series of Instagram posts promoting a new fitness app."

2. Focus on engagement: "Include tips, user testimonials, and interactive challenges to engage followers."

3. Review and adjust based on engagement metrics.

Exercise 18: Crafting Press Releases

Objective: Use AI to write professional press releases.
Instructions:

1. Write a prompt for a press release: "Write a press release announcing the launch of a new electric vehicle."

2.Include key details: "Highlight the vehicle's features, launch date, and market impact."

3. Refine the press release for clarity and impact.

Exercise 19: Generating Creative Content

Objective: Use AI to generate creative content for various media.
Instructions:
1. Write a prompt for a poem: "Write a poem about the beauty of nature."
2. Include specific themes: "Incorporate themes of renewal and tranquility."
3. Experiment with different styles and refine based on the desired tone and imagery.

Exercise 20: Creating Training Materials

Objective: Craft prompts to generate training materials for professional development.
Instructions:
1. Write a prompt for a training module: "Develop a training module for new employees on workplace safety."
2. Include interactive elements: "Incorporate quizzes and real-life scenarios to enhance learning."
3. Review and adjust for clarity and engagement.

Exercise 21: Developing Business Plans
Objective: Use AI to draft comprehensive business plans.
Instructions:
1. Write a prompt for a business plan: "Draft a business plan for a startup focused on renewable energy solutions."
2. Include detailed sections: "Cover market analysis, financial projections, and marketing strategies."
3. Refine the plan based on feedback and additional research.

Exercise 22: Writing Personal Essays

Objective: Use AI to assist in writing personal essays and statements.

Instructions:

1. Write a prompt for a personal essay: "Write a personal statement for a college application."

2. Include key themes: "Discuss your academic achievements, career goals, and personal motivations."

3. Refine the essay to ensure it is compelling and reflective of personal experiences.

Exercise 23: Analyzing Competitive Landscapes

Objective: Use AI to analyze competitive landscapes in various industries.

Instructions:

1. Write a prompt for competitive analysis: "Analyze the competitive landscape of the e-commerce industry."

2. Focus on specific aspects: "Identify key players, market share, and recent trends."

3. Refine the analysis to provide strategic insights.

Exercise 24: Crafting Grant Proposals

Objective: Use AI to write effective grant proposals.

Instructions:

1. Write a prompt for a grant proposal: "Draft a grant proposal for a community health initiative."

2. Include essential components: "Outline the project's objectives, methods, and expected outcomes."

3. Review and refine to ensure clarity and persuasiveness.

Exercise 25: Creating User Guides

Objective: Use AI to generate comprehensive user guides.

Instructions:

1. Write a prompt for a user guide: "Create a user guide for a new software application."

2. Include detailed instructions: "Provide step-by-step setup, usage tips, and troubleshooting advice."

3. Refine the guide for clarity and user-friendliness.

Exercise 26: Conducting Surveys and Polls

Objective: Use AI to design effective surveys and polls.

Instructions:

1. Write a prompt for a survey: "Create a survey to gather customer feedback on a new product."

2. Include relevant questions: "Focus on product satisfaction, usability, and improvement suggestions."

3. Review and adjust for comprehensiveness and clarity.

Exercise 27: Writing Research Summaries

Objective: Use AI to summarize complex research papers.

Instructions:

1. Write a prompt for a research summary: "Summarize the findings of a recent study on climate change impacts on agriculture."

2. Highlight key points: "Include the study's methodology, results, and implications."

3. Refine the summary for accuracy and conciseness.

Exercise 28: Developing Case Studies

Objective: Use AI to develop detailed case studies.

Instructions:

1. Write a prompt for a case study: "Develop a case study on a successful digital marketing campaign."

2. Include key elements: "Describe the campaign strategy, implementation, and measurable outcomes."

3. Review and refine to ensure it is informative and engaging.

Exercise 29: Creating Event Agendas

Objective: Use AI to draft detailed event agendas.

Instructions:

1. Write a prompt for an event agenda: "Create an agenda for a one-day corporate training workshop."

2. Include session details: "Outline the schedule, topics, and speakers for each session."

3. Refine the agenda for clarity and comprehensiveness.

Exercise 30: Generating Personalized Learning Plans

Objective: Use AI to develop personalized learning plans.

Instructions:

1. Write a prompt for a learning plan: "Develop a personalized learning plan for a high school student struggling with math."

2. Include specific goals: "Set objectives for improving algebra and geometry skills through targeted practice and tutoring."

3. Review and refine to ensure it meets the student's needs and learning style.

By engaging in these step-by-step exercises, you can systematically develop and refine your prompt crafting skills. These practical tasks not only enhance your ability to interact effectively with GPT-4 but also build a solid foundation for advanced prompt engineering techniques, ensuring you achieve the best possible results in your AI-driven projects.

4.4 Challenge Yourself: Advanced Prompt Scenarios

Ready for a challenge? Advanced prompt scenarios are designed to test your skills and push your limits, helping you master the art of prompt crafting. These exercises require a deeper understanding of GPT-4's capabilities and a strategic approach to get the best results. Try these advanced scenarios to see how well you can apply what you've learned and take your prompt crafting skills to the next level.

Scenario 1: Multi-Disciplinary Research Paper

Objective: Integrate knowledge from various fields to generate a comprehensive research paper.

Instructions:

1. Write a prompt to draft an interdisciplinary research paper: "Write a research paper on the impact of climate change on global food security, integrating perspectives from agriculture, economics, and environmental science."

2. Ensure each section is detailed and coherent.

3. Refine the paper for academic quality and clarity.

Scenario 2: Creative World-Building

Objective: Develop a richly detailed fictional world for a novel or game.

Instructions:

1. Write a prompt to create a detailed world: "Develop a fantasy world, including geography, politics, cultures, and magic systems."

2. Include prompts for specific aspects: "Describe the political system of the central kingdom," "Detail the unique magical creatures found in the northern forests."

3. Ensure consistency and depth across all elements.

Scenario 3: Legal Document Drafting

Objective: Generate a legally sound and detailed document.
Instructions:
1. Write a prompt to draft a legal contract: "Draft a non-disclosure agreement (NDA) for a tech startup, ensuring it covers confidentiality, terms of agreement, and penalties for breaches."
2. Review the document for legal terminology and thoroughness.
3. Refine for accuracy and completeness.

Scenario 4: Advanced Data Analysis Report

Objective: Perform a complex data analysis and generate a detailed report.
Instructions:

1. Write a prompt to analyze a dataset: "Analyze the provided dataset on global internet usage trends and generate a detailed report, including visualizations and key insights."
2. Specify the types of analyses: "Conduct a time series analysis to identify trends over the past decade."
3. Review the report for clarity, accuracy, and depth of analysis.

Scenario 5: Multi-Language Content Creation

Objective: Create content that is accurate and culturally relevant in multiple languages.
Instructions:
1. Write a prompt to generate marketing content: "Create a marketing campaign for a new fitness app, with advertisements in English, Spanish, and Mandarin, tailored to each culture."
2. Ensure the content is culturally appropriate and engaging.
3. Review for language accuracy and cultural nuances.

Scenario 6: Comprehensive Business Strategy Plan

Objective: Develop a detailed and strategic business plan.
Instructions:
1. Write a prompt to draft a business strategy: "Develop a comprehensive business strategy for a new e-commerce platform, including market analysis, competitive strategy, operational plan, and financial projections."
2. Ensure each section is thorough and cohesive.
3. Refine for strategic clarity and feasibility.

Scenario 7: Historical Fiction Narrative

Objective: Write a compelling historical fiction story with accurate historical details.
Instructions:
1. Write a prompt to develop a narrative: "Write a historical fiction short story set in Victorian London, focusing on a young detective solving a mystery."
2. Include historically accurate details and vivid descriptions.
3. Ensure the narrative is engaging and historically credible.

Scenario 8: Detailed Scientific Report

Objective: Generate a scientifically accurate and detailed report.
Instructions:
1. Write a prompt to draft a report: "Write a detailed scientific report on the effects of microplastics in marine ecosystems."
2. Include sections on methodology, findings, and implications.
3. Review for scientific accuracy and thoroughness.

Scenario 9: Personalized Learning Curriculum

Objective: Create a tailored educational curriculum for diverse learning needs.

Instructions:

1. Write a prompt to develop a curriculum: "Create a personalized learning curriculum for a high school student struggling with math and science, including daily lesson plans and interactive activities."

2. Ensure the curriculum addresses individual learning styles and needs.

3. Refine for clarity, engagement, and effectiveness.

Scenario 10: Strategic Marketing Analysis

Objective: Conduct an in-depth marketing analysis for a product launch.

Instructions:

1. Write a prompt to analyze the market: "Conduct a strategic marketing analysis for launching a new electric vehicle, including target audience, competitive analysis, and marketing strategies."

2. Ensure the analysis is detailed and actionable.

3. Review for strategic insight and market relevance.

Scenario 11: Detailed Code Documentation

Objective: Generate comprehensive documentation for a complex software project.

Instructions:

1. Write a prompt to document a software project: "Create detailed documentation for a new open-source software library, including installation instructions, API reference, and usage examples."

2. Ensure the documentation is clear and thorough.

3. Refine for technical accuracy and usability.

Scenario 12: Crisis Management Plan

Objective: Develop a detailed crisis management plan for a business.
Instructions:

1. Write a prompt to draft a crisis plan: "Develop a comprehensive crisis management plan for a retail company, including risk assessment, communication strategy, and recovery plan."
2. Ensure the plan covers all potential scenarios and responses.
3. Review for completeness and practicality.

Scenario 13: Multi-Stage Project Proposal

Objective: Create a detailed proposal for a multi-stage project.

Instructions:
1. Write a prompt to develop a proposal: "Create a detailed project proposal for developing a new community park, including planning, funding, construction, and community engagement stages."
2. Ensure each stage is well-defined and feasible.
3. Refine for clarity and persuasiveness.

Scenario 14: Advanced Literary Analysis

Objective: Perform a detailed literary analysis of a complex text.
Instructions:
1. Write a prompt to analyze a literary work: "Conduct a detailed literary analysis of 'Moby-Dick,' focusing on themes, character development, and symbolism."
2. Ensure the analysis is deep and insightful.
3. Review for academic rigor and clarity.

Scenario 15: In-Depth Industry Report

Objective: Generate a comprehensive report on an industry.

Instructions:

1. Write a prompt to draft an industry report: "Write a comprehensive report on the renewable energy industry, including market trends, key players, and future prospects."

2. Ensure the report is detailed and well-researched.

3. Refine for accuracy and strategic insight.

Scenario 16: Detailed Historical Analysis

Objective: Conduct an in-depth analysis of a historical event.

Instructions:

1. Write a prompt to analyze a historical event: "Analyze the causes and consequences of the French Revolution, focusing on social, economic, and political factors."

2. Ensure the analysis is thorough and well-supported by historical evidence.

3. Review for clarity and depth.

Scenario 17: Advanced Creative Collaboration

Objective: Use AI to co-create a complex creative work.

Instructions:

1. Write a prompt to develop a collaborative work: "Co-write a science fiction screenplay with detailed scenes, dialogue, and character arcs."

2. Ensure the screenplay is cohesive and engaging.

3. Refine for narrative flow and creative depth.

Scenario 18: Comprehensive Policy Analysis

Objective: Generate a detailed analysis of a public policy.

Instructions:

1. Write a prompt to analyze a policy: "Conduct a comprehensive analysis of the impact of universal healthcare on the US economy and public health."

2. Include sections on economic impact, health outcomes, and policy implementation.

3. Review for thoroughness and policy relevance.

Scenario 19: Detailed Architectural Plan

Objective: Develop a comprehensive architectural plan for a complex structure.

Instructions:

1. Write a prompt to create an architectural plan: "Develop a detailed architectural plan for a sustainable office building, including design, materials, and energy efficiency features."

2. Ensure the plan is innovative and feasible.

3. Refine for clarity and technical accuracy.

Scenario 20: Advanced Financial Analysis

Objective: Perform a detailed financial analysis for a business.

Instructions:

1. Write a prompt to analyze financial data: "Conduct a detailed financial analysis for a tech startup, including profitability, cash flow, and investment potential."

2. Ensure the analysis is comprehensive and insightful.

3. Review for accuracy and strategic value.

By challenging yourself with these advanced scenarios, you can push the boundaries of your prompt crafting skills and deepen your understanding of GPT-4's capabilities. These exercises not only test your ability to create effective prompts but also enhance your proficiency in handling complex tasks and generating high-quality outputs.

4.5 Adaptive Learning Prompts

daptive learning prompts are an advanced technique that allows your interactions with GPT-4 to evolve based on user feedback and the AI's responses. This approach is essential for continuous improvement, enabling you to refine and optimize prompts over time to achieve better outcomes. In this section, you'll learn how to create adaptive learning prompts that adjust dynamically, ensuring that your AI-driven projects remain relevant, effective, and finely tuned.

Understanding Adaptive Learning: Adaptive learning involves creating prompts that can change and improve based on feedback. This iterative process is key to refining your prompts and achieving more accurate and relevant responses from GPT-4.

Incorporating Feedback Loops: To create adaptive learning prompts, integrate feedback mechanisms that allow you to assess and adjust the prompts based on the AI's performance and user responses.

Example Prompt: "Generate a summary of this article on climate change. If the summary is too technical, simplify it to be more accessible for high school students."

Feedback Loop: Review the initial summary and provide feedback. Adjust the prompt based on whether the summary was too complex or too simple.

Analyzing AI Responses: Examine the responses from GPT-4 to identify patterns, strengths, and weaknesses. Use this analysis to refine your prompts, making them more precise and tailored to your needs.

Example Prompt: "Explain the economic impact of renewable energy adoption. If the response lacks depth, ask for a more detailed analysis with specific examples."

Analysis: If the initial response is superficial, adjust the prompt to request deeper insights and concrete examples.

User-Centric Adjustments: Incorporate user feedback directly into your prompt crafting process. This ensures that the content generated by GPT-4 meets the expectations and needs of the end-users.

Example Prompt: "Create a customer satisfaction survey. After deployment, refine the questions based on user feedback to ensure they are clear and relevant."

Adjustment: If users find certain questions confusing, adjust the prompt to clarify or rephrase those questions.

Dynamic Content Generation: Use adaptive prompts to generate content that evolves in real-time based on ongoing interactions. This is particularly useful for applications like chatbots and interactive learning modules.

Example Prompt: "Develop a chatbot script for customer service. Continuously refine the script based on customer interactions and common queries."

Dynamic Adjustment: If certain responses are frequently misunderstood, adjust the script to provide clearer, more informative answers.

Iterative Refinement Process: Adopt an iterative refinement process where each prompt is a version that improves upon the previous one. Document the changes and their impacts to understand what works best.

Example Prompt: "Write an introductory guide to machine learning. After reviewing the first draft, provide feedback and request specific improvements for clarity and detail."

Refinement: Each subsequent version incorporates feedback to enhance the guide's clarity and comprehensiveness.

Leveraging Analytics Tools: Utilize analytics tools to track the performance of your prompts. Metrics such as user engagement, completion rates, and feedback scores can guide your adjustments.

Example Prompt: "Generate content for an online course on digital marketing. Use analytics to monitor which modules are most engaging and refine the prompts accordingly."

Analytics: If a particular module has low engagement, adjust the prompt to make the content more interactive and engaging.

Personalizing Learning Experiences: Create adaptive learning prompts that cater to individual learning styles and preferences. This personalization can significantly enhance the effectiveness of educational content.

Example Prompt: "Develop personalized learning exercises for a language learning app, adapting difficulty based on user performance."
Personalization: If a user consistently excels, increase the difficulty level in subsequent exercises; if they struggle, provide additional support and simpler tasks.

Continuous Improvement Framework: Establish a continuous improvement framework where adaptive learning prompts are regularly reviewed and updated based on the latest data and user feedback.

Example Prompt: "Maintain a knowledge base for a tech support team. Regularly update the content based on user queries and feedback."

Framework: Schedule regular reviews and updates to ensure the knowledge base remains accurate and comprehensive.

Real-Time Adjustments: For real-time applications, create prompts that adjust dynamically based on immediate feedback and context changes.

Example Prompt: "Develop a real-time interactive quiz for a virtual classroom. Adjust the difficulty and hints based on student performance during the session."

Real-Time Adjustment: If students find a question particularly challenging, the AI can provide additional hints or simplify the question in real-time.

By mastering adaptive learning prompts, you can ensure that your AI interactions are continuously evolving and improving. This approach not only enhances the accuracy and relevance of the AI's responses but also ensures that your content and interactions remain engaging and effective over time. Embrace the principles of adaptive learning to achieve ongoing refinement and excellence in your AI-driven projects.

4.6 Personalized AI Interactions

In the world of AI, personalization is key to creating meaningful and effective interactions. By tailoring AI responses to suit individual preferences and needs, you can enhance user experience, increase engagement, and achieve more precise results. This section will guide you on how to create personalized AI interactions using GPT-4, focusing on customizing content and solutions to match specific requirements and preferences.

Understanding Personalization: Personalization involves adapting the AI's responses to align with the unique preferences, needs, and contexts of the user. This process enhances the relevance and effectiveness of the interactions, making the AI more useful and engaging.

Collecting User Preferences: The first step in personalization is to gather relevant information about the user's preferences, interests, and needs. This data forms the basis for tailoring responses and content.

Example Prompt: "Develop a user profile for a language learning app. Ask the user about their preferred language, learning style, and goals."

Data Collection: Use the collected information to customize lessons, exercises, and feedback to better suit the user's learning journey.

Customizing Content Based on Preferences: Once you have user data, you can customize the content to match their preferences. This could involve adjusting the tone, style, complexity, and focus of the responses.

Example Prompt: "Create a personalized news summary for a user interested in technology, business, and sports. Adjust the tone to be informal and engaging."

Customization: Ensure the content is relevant to the user's interests and presented in a style they find appealing.

Adaptive Learning and Interaction: Personalized AI interactions can adapt over time based on the user's progress, feedback, and changing preferences. This dynamic adjustment ensures the content remains relevant and effective.

Example Prompt: "Develop a personalized workout plan for a user. Adapt the exercises based on their progress and feedback, gradually increasing the difficulty as they improve."

Adaptation: Regularly update the workout plan to reflect the user's development and goals.

Leveraging Contextual Information: Contextual information such as location, time of day, and recent activities can enhance personalization by making interactions more timely and relevant.

Example Prompt: "Provide personalized travel tips for a user visiting Paris, including recommendations for restaurants, attractions, and activities based on the weather and time of day."

Contextualization: Use real-time data to tailor the recommendations, ensuring they are practical and timely.

Creating Personalized Communication Styles: Tailor the communication style of the AI to match the user's preferences, whether they prefer formal, casual, humorous, or straightforward interactions.

Example Prompt: "Write a personalized email response to a customer complaint. Use a professional tone and address the customer's specific concerns about delayed shipping."

Style Adjustment: Match the tone and style to the context and user's expectations to enhance satisfaction.

Incorporating Feedback for Continuous Improvement: Encourage users to provide feedback on the AI's responses and use this feedback to continuously improve and refine the personalization.

Example Prompt: "After providing a product recommendation, ask the user for feedback on the relevance and usefulness of the suggestion. Adjust future recommendations based on their input."

Feedback Loop: Use the feedback to fine-tune the AI's responses, making them more aligned with the user's needs.

Dynamic Personalization in Real-Time Applications: For applications requiring real-time interaction, such as chatbots and virtual assistants, implement dynamic personalization that adjusts instantly based on the user's input.

Example Prompt: "Develop a real-time chatbot for a financial services website. Personalize the interaction based on the user's account history, recent transactions, and queries."

Real-Time Adjustment: Ensure the chatbot can dynamically adjust its responses to provide accurate and relevant assistance.

Creating Segmented Personalization Strategies: For larger user bases, segment users into groups based on shared characteristics and preferences. This approach allows for scalable yet personalized interactions.

Example Prompt: "Segment users of an online shopping platform based on their purchase history and preferences. Create personalized product recommendations for each segment."

Segmentation: Develop targeted content and recommendations that cater to the specific needs of each user group.

Enhancing User Experience through Personalization: The ultimate goal of personalized AI interactions is to enhance the overall user experience, making interactions more engaging, relevant, and satisfying.

Example Prompt: "Design a personalized onboarding experience for new users of a software application. Tailor the tutorial content to match the user's background and expertise level."

Experience Enhancement: Ensure the onboarding process is smooth and tailored to the user's unique profile, improving their initial engagement and satisfaction.

By mastering the techniques of personalized AI interactions, you can create more meaningful and effective engagements with GPT-4. These personalized interactions not only enhance user satisfaction but also drive better outcomes in various applications, from education and customer service to marketing and personal development. Embrace personalization to deliver tailored solutions that resonate with individual users and address their specific needs.

4.7 Collaborative Prompt Crafting

Collaborative prompt crafting is an essential strategy for teams working with AI like GPT-4. It combines the diverse skills and perspectives of various team members to create more effective, comprehensive, and nuanced prompts. This approach not only enhances the quality of the prompts but also ensures that the responses from AI are more accurate and tailored to the project's needs. In this section, we'll explore how teams can work together to craft effective prompts, highlighting best practices and collaborative techniques.

Benefits of Collaborative Prompt Crafting: Collaboration in prompt crafting brings together different viewpoints, ensuring a more rounded approach to problem-solving. It helps in identifying potential biases, gaps in logic, or areas where the prompt may not be clear enough, thereby refining the final outcome.

Establishing Clear Objectives: Before beginning the prompt crafting process, it's crucial for the team to clearly define what they hope to achieve with the AI's responses. This common understanding guides the direction of the prompt and ensures all team members are aligned.

- **Example Activity:** Conduct a brainstorming session to outline the goals of the AI interaction, such as generating a report, analyzing data, or automating a task.

Diverse Team Involvement: Incorporate team members from different disciplines such as technical experts, content creators, and project managers. Each member brings unique insights that contribute to creating a well-rounded prompt.

- **Example Activity:** Hold a workshop where each team member can provide input on their specific expertise area, discussing how the AI can best address the needs of their department.

Iterative Development Process: Prompt crafting should be an iterative process where initial drafts are continuously refined based on team feedback and test outputs from the AI.

-**Example Activity:** Use a shared document or a collaboration tool where team members can edit the prompt, add comments, and suggest improvements. After each iteration, test the prompt with GPT-4 and review the output collectively.

Utilizing Specialized Knowledge: Leverage the specialized knowledge of team members to add depth and accuracy to the prompts. Technical experts can ensure that the prompts are precise and based on sound knowledge, while creative team members can enhance the readability and engagement of the text.

-**Example Activity:** Assign roles where technical members focus on the accuracy of content, and creative members work on the language and presentation of the prompt.

Feedback Mechanisms: Implement a robust feedback system where responses from GPT-4 are evaluated critically by the team. This helps in pinpointing areas where the prompt needs refinement.

-Example Activity: Regularly schedule review meetings to discuss AI outputs and gather feedback from all team members. Use this feedback to make targeted improvements to the prompts.

Training Sessions: Conduct training sessions for team members to understand the best practices in prompt crafting and the capabilities and limitations of GPT-4. This shared knowledge base will improve the quality of collaborative efforts.

-Example Activity: Organize a training workshop led by an AI expert who can provide insights into effective prompt crafting strategies and the latest developments in AI technology.

Documentation and Standardization: Document successful prompts and establish guidelines for different types of prompt crafting scenarios. This repository can serve as a valuable resource for the team, helping to standardize prompt crafting across the organization.

-Example Activity: Create a digital library of successful prompts and guidelines that can be accessed by the team for future projects. Include case studies and examples where specific prompts have led to successful outcomes.

Monitoring and Evaluation: Continuously monitor the effectiveness of the collaborative prompt crafting process and make adjustments as necessary. Evaluation should be based on specific metrics such as the quality of AI responses, the efficiency of the process, and the satisfaction of team members.

- **Example Activity:** Implement a quarterly review process to assess the impact of collaborative prompt crafting on project outcomes and team productivity.

By fostering a collaborative environment for prompt crafting, teams can leverage their collective expertise to produce superior prompts that yield more effective and reliable results from GPT-4. This cooperative approach not only enhances the quality of the AI interactions but also encourages a culture of continuous learning and improvement within the team.

4.8 Personal Feedback Integration: Enhancing AI Interactions

Incorporating personal feedback into AI interactions is a crucial strategy for enhancing the effectiveness and personalization of AI-generated content. This refocused approach emphasizes how individual users can continuously improve their prompt crafting skills and refine AI responses based on their own experiences and observations. This section will explore methods for integrating personal feedback, ensuring that each user can optimize their interaction with AI without necessarily relying on a broader community.

The Importance of Personal Feedback: Personal feedback is direct input from individual users about their experiences with AI-generated responses. It allows users to tailor AI interactions to better meet their specific needs and preferences, leading to more relevant and effective outcomes.

Setting Up Feedback Mechanisms: To effectively integrate personal feedback, users need to establish simple mechanisms for capturing their reactions and thoughts during AI interactions.
- **Example Activity:** Implement a practice of maintaining a feedback journal where notes on AI responses can be recorded, including what worked well and what didn't.

Reflective Practice: Encourage users to engage in reflective practice, where they periodically review their AI interactions and feedback to identify patterns, strengths, and areas for improvement.
- **Example Activity:** Schedule weekly review sessions to go through interactions and feedback, focusing on refining prompts and response expectations based on past outcomes.

Customizing Prompts Based on Feedback: Use insights gained from personal feedback to customize and refine prompts. This ensures that the AI better understands the context and delivers responses that are more aligned with the user's needs.

-Example Activity: If feedback indicates that responses are too technical, adjust the prompts to request simpler explanations or definitions.

Adaptive Prompt Strategies: Develop adaptive prompt strategies that evolve based on ongoing feedback. This approach allows users to fine-tune how they communicate with the AI, leading to progressively better interactions.
-Example Activity: Create a set of variable prompts that can be adjusted based on the effectiveness of previous interactions, such as changing the level of detail requested or the complexity of the language used.

Iterative Learning: Highlight the iterative nature of learning with AI. Encourage users to view each interaction as an opportunity to learn and improve both their understanding of the subject matter and their ability to craft effective prompts.
-Example Activity: Implement a loop of action, reflection, and revision where users actively test different prompts, observe the results, and make necessary adjustments.

Documenting Improvements: Maintain detailed records of how personal feedback has led to changes in AI interactions and the benefits of these changes. This not only tracks progress but also motivates continued engagement and refinement.
-Example Activity: Keep a log or digital record of prompts before and after adjustments, noting changes in AI performance and user satisfaction.

Sharing Best Practices: While this approach focuses on individual feedback, sharing personal best practices within a team or community can still be beneficial. Encourage users to share their most effective prompts and feedback strategies with peers.
-Example Activity: Create a shared digital space where users can post their most successful prompts and the specific changes they made based on their feedback, allowing others to learn from their experiences.

By focusing on personal feedback integration, users can take a more active role in shaping their AI interactions. This hands-on approach not only enhances the relevance and effectiveness of AI responses but also empowers users to become adept at managing AI tools to suit their specific needs and goals. This proactive engagement leads to a deeper understanding of both the potential and limitations of AI, fostering a more productive and satisfying user experience.

Chapter 5

Advanced Topics:

5.1 Exploring Advanced Prompt Design Theories:

I n this chapter, we dive deep into the theories behind advanced prompt design, exploring concepts that can significantly enhance your ability to craft effective prompts. Understanding these advanced techniques will take your skills to the next level, enabling you to leverage the full potential of large language models (LLMs) like GPT-4. We'll cover key theories and techniques such as backpropagation, zero-shot and few-shot learning, transfer learning, and prompt adaptation.

Advanced Learning Techniques in LLMs

1. Backpropagation and its Role in LLMs

Understanding Backpropagation: Backpropagation is a fundamental algorithm used in training neural networks, including large language models. It involves calculating the gradient of the loss function with respect to each weight by the chain rule, allowing the model to adjust its weights and reduce errors during training.

Theory: Backpropagation helps the model learn from errors by iteratively updating the weights. This process continues until the model reaches a point where it can predict outputs with high accuracy.

Application: When crafting prompts, understanding backpropagation can help you appreciate how the model has been trained to respond to different inputs. Knowing that the model has learned from vast datasets and refined its predictions through countless iterations can guide you in creating more precise and effective prompts.

Practical Example: Imagine you're trying to generate technical documentation for a new software tool. By recognizing that the model has been trained using backpropagation on numerous examples of technical writing, you can craft your prompt to align with the language and structure it has learned.

Example Prompt: "Write an introduction for a user manual on a new project management software, including features and benefits."

2. Zero-shot Learning and Few-shot Learning

Zero-shot Learning: Zero-shot learning refers to the model's ability to understand and perform tasks it has not explicitly been trained on. It relies on the model's general understanding of language and context to generate relevant responses.

Theory: Zero-shot learning leverages the model's broad training to make inferences about new, unseen tasks. This is particularly useful when you need the model to handle novel scenarios without specific training data.

Application: Craft prompts that clearly define the task and provide enough context for the model to generate appropriate responses, even if it hasn't encountered similar tasks before.

Practical Example: If you want GPT-4 to write a poem in a specific style it hasn't been trained on, you can use zero-shot learning by providing detailed instructions and context.

Example Prompt: "Write a poem in the style of Emily Dickinson about the beauty of nature."

Few-shot Learning: Few-shot learning involves providing the model with a few examples of the desired output to help it understand the task better. This method bridges the gap between zero-shot learning and full training on large datasets.

Theory: By showing the model a few examples, you can guide its responses more effectively. This technique is beneficial for more complex tasks where context and format are crucial.

Application: Use few-shot learning to provide the model with examples that illustrate the desired structure and content.

Practical Example: When creating a business proposal, you can give the model a few example sections to help it understand the format and tone you're looking for.

Example Prompt: "Write an executive summary for a business proposal. Here are a few examples to guide you: [provide examples]."

3. Transfer Learning and Prompt Adaptation

Transfer Learning: Transfer learning involves leveraging a pre-trained model on a new, related task. The model retains knowledge from the initial training and applies it to solve new problems more efficiently.

Theory: Transfer learning allows the model to build on existing knowledge, reducing the need for extensive training on new tasks. This technique is particularly powerful in adapting LLMs to specific domains or tasks.

Application: Use transfer learning to fine-tune GPT-4 for specific applications, such as medical writing or legal analysis, by providing domain-specific examples and context.

Practical Example: If you're using GPT-4 to generate medical reports, you can fine-tune it by providing medical texts and examples, enabling the model to produce more accurate and relevant content.

Example Prompt: "Generate a summary of a patient's medical history, including diagnosis, treatment, and follow-up recommendations. Here are some examples to guide you: [provide examples]."

Prompt Adaptation: Prompt adaptation involves adjusting prompts based on the model's previous responses and the specific requirements of the task. This iterative process ensures that the model's outputs are continuously refined and aligned with user expectations.

Theory: By adapting prompts iteratively, you can enhance the relevance and accuracy of the AI's responses. This process involves analyzing previous outputs and modifying prompts to better meet the desired outcomes.

Application: Continuously refine your prompts based on feedback and results to improve the quality of AI interactions.

Practical Example: When developing educational content, start with a general prompt and iteratively adapt it based on the responses to ensure clarity and engagement.

Example Prompt: "Create a lesson plan for a high school biology class on the topic of cellular respiration. Start with an introduction, then explain the process in detail, and include interactive activities."

By understanding and applying these advanced prompt design theories, you can significantly enhance your ability to craft effective prompts that leverage the full potential of GPT-4. These techniques not only improve the accuracy and relevance of AI responses but also empower you to tackle complex tasks with greater confidence and precision.

5.2 Troubleshooting Common Prompt Issues and Getting Better Results

Creating effective prompts is an essential skill for maximizing the utility of large language models like GPT-4. However, even experienced users can encounter issues that reduce the effectiveness of their prompts. This section will explore common prompt-related problems and provide strategies for troubleshooting and refining prompts to achieve better results.

Identifying Common Prompt Issues: Several typical issues can arise when crafting prompts for AI interaction:

1. **Vagueness and Ambiguity:** Prompts that are too vague or ambiguous can lead to irrelevant or overly broad responses.
2. **Over-specification:** Conversely, prompts that are overly detailed or complex can restrict the AI's responses, preventing it from providing useful additional information.
3. **Misalignment with AI Capabilities:** Prompts that ask for information or tasks beyond the AI's current capabilities or training can result in inaccurate or nonsensical answers.
4. **Inappropriate Tone or Style:** Prompts that don't match the desired tone or style can lead to content that feels out of place for the intended audience.

Example Prompts and Troubleshooting Strategies:

Issue: Vagueness and Ambiguity

Original Prompt: "Tell me about dogs."
Revised Prompt: "Provide a detailed overview of the evolution, behavior, and care of domestic dogs."
Strategy: Specify what aspects of dogs are of interest to narrow down the focus and provide more detailed, relevant content.

Issue: Over-specification

Original Prompt: "Write a 500-word essay on the economic impact of renewable energy by discussing wind turbines, solar panels, renewable energy policies in Europe, tax incentives in the US, and global warming implications."
Revised Prompt: "Write a 500-word essay on the economic impact of renewable energy focusing on key factors such as government policies and technological advances."

Strategy: Simplify the prompt to focus on broader categories, allowing the AI to naturally select the most relevant information without being constrained by too many specifics.

Issue: Misalignment with AI Capabilities

Original Prompt: "Predict stock market prices for the next year."
Revised Prompt: "Summarize recent trends in the stock market and discuss factors that can influence future market conditions."
Strategy: Reframe the prompt to focus on generating information-based responses that are within the AI's capabilities rather than expecting predictive analysis which is highly speculative.

Issue: Inappropriate Tone or Style

Original Prompt: "Write a casual blog post about recent scientific discoveries in space."
Revised Prompt: "Write an informative and engaging blog post suitable for science enthusiasts about recent discoveries in space exploration."
Strategy: Specify the audience and desired tone to align the style of the content with the expectations of the readers.

Implementing Feedback Loops:

Incorporate feedback mechanisms to continuously refine prompts based on the quality of the AI's responses. User feedback can particularly be valuable in understanding how well the AI's output meets the intended needs.

Example Activity: After receiving AI-generated content, solicit feedback from users on its relevance and usefulness. Use this feedback to adjust prompts and improve future responses.

Testing and Iteration: A key strategy in troubleshooting is the iterative testing of prompts. By systematically varying aspects of the prompt and observing the changes in the AI's responses, you can better understand how different prompt formulations affect output.

Example Activity: Conduct A/B testing with different prompt variations to determine which produces more accurate and relevant responses. For instance, test different levels of specificity or various phrasing styles to see which yields better results.

Documenting Best Practices: Keep a record of successful prompts and the conditions under which they were effective. This documentation can serve as a valuable reference for crafting future prompts and training other team members.

Example Activity: Create a 'Prompt Playbook' that includes examples of well-crafted prompts along with notes on why they were effective and how similar strategies can be applied to new content needs.

By understanding common prompt issues and implementing these troubleshooting strategies, you can significantly improve the effectiveness of your interactions with AI models like GPT-4. This not only ensures higher quality outputs but also enhances the efficiency of your AI-driven projects, enabling you to leverage AI technology to its fullest potential.

5.3 The Future of Prompt Design and Emerging Trends

As AI technology continues to evolve, so does the art and science of prompt design. In this section, we'll explore the latest trends and future directions in prompt design, offering insights into how you can stay ahead of the curve and enhance your skills for the evolving landscape of AI interactions.

Emerging Trends in Prompt Design:

1. Contextual Understanding and Adaptation:
Trend: Advances in natural language processing (NLP) are pushing AI to better understand context and adapt responses dynamically. Future prompts will leverage this capability to maintain coherence and relevance across longer interactions.
Example: Develop prompts that guide the AI to refer back to previous parts of the conversation, ensuring that responses remain relevant and

coherent. For instance, "Based on our previous discussion about renewable energy, can you expand on the economic impacts of solar power in developing countries?"

2. Integration of Multimodal Inputs:

Trend: The integration of text, image, video, and audio inputs is becoming more prevalent, enabling AI to generate more comprehensive and contextually rich responses.

Example: Create prompts that include multimodal elements, such as "Describe the scene in the image attached, including possible cultural and historical contexts," or "Generate a summary of this video transcript focusing on the key points discussed."

3. Interactive and Iterative Prompting:

Trend: Future prompt design will increasingly incorporate interactive elements, allowing users to refine and adjust prompts in real-time based on AI feedback.

Example: Implement prompts that invite user interaction, such as "Refine the previous response by adding more details on the social implications of the findings. What additional information would enhance the discussion?"

4. Personalization and User-Centric Design:

Trend: AI will become more adept at personalizing interactions based on user preferences, history, and behavior, making prompts more tailored and effective.

Example: Design prompts that adjust based on user profiles, such as "Considering your previous interests in AI ethics, provide an analysis of the latest developments in AI bias mitigation techniques."

5. Ethical and Responsible AI Prompts:

Trend: There is a growing emphasis on developing prompts that promote ethical behavior and reduce biases in AI responses. This includes ensuring that prompts are designed to avoid harmful or misleading content.

Example: Craft prompts with built-in ethical guidelines, such as "Generate a response to this question while ensuring it respects privacy, avoids stereotypes, and promotes inclusivity."

Future Directions in Prompt Design:

1. Advanced Prompt Engineering Tools:

Development: Expect the emergence of more sophisticated tools and platforms designed specifically for prompt engineering, offering features like AI-driven suggestions, performance analytics, and real-time feedback.

Example: Use platforms like Promptor or OpenAI Playground to experiment with new prompt structures and analyze their effectiveness through detailed metrics.

2. Cross-Disciplinary Innovations:

Trend: The fusion of AI with fields such as psychology, linguistics, and cognitive science will lead to more nuanced and effective prompt designs that consider human cognition and behavior.

Example: Design prompts based on cognitive principles, such as "Explain this concept as you would to a five-year-old, focusing on simple language and relatable examples."

3. Enhanced AI Training Techniques:

Development: Innovations in AI training methodologies, such as few-shot and zero-shot learning, will continue to advance, enabling models to handle a wider range of prompts with minimal prior training.

Example: Experiment with prompts that test the model's ability to generalize from few examples, like "Based on the following examples, generate a list of potential challenges in AI ethics."

4. Collaborative and Community-Driven Prompt Development:

Trend: There will be an increasing focus on community-driven approaches to prompt design, where users collaboratively share, test, and refine prompts, fostering a global exchange of ideas and best practices.

Example: Engage in community platforms or forums dedicated to prompt engineering, such as those found on GitHub or AI research communities, to share your prompts and gain insights from others.

5. Exploration of New Application Areas:

Development: As AI capabilities expand, new application areas for prompt design will emerge, from healthcare and legal advice to creative arts and scientific research.

Example: Develop prompts tailored to emerging fields, such as "Generate a research proposal on the ethical implications of AI in healthcare, considering patient privacy and data security."

Staying Ahead in Prompt Design:

Continuous Learning: Keep up with the latest research papers, attend webinars, and participate in workshops related to AI and prompt design.

Experimentation: Regularly test new ideas and variations in your prompts, using feedback and performance metrics to refine your approaches.

Collaboration: Join online communities, attend meetups, and engage with other prompt designers to exchange ideas, solve challenges, and stay inspired.

By embracing these emerging trends and future directions, you can enhance your prompt design skills, making your interactions with AI models like GPT-4 more effective, innovative, and impactful. Whether you're exploring new creative avenues, developing cutting-edge applications, or simply enhancing your everyday interactions with AI, the future of prompt design offers exciting possibilities for growth and discovery.

5.4 Ethical Considerations in Using and Advancing LLMs

E thics in AI is a multifaceted issue that becomes even more critical with the advanced functionalities of large language models (LLMs) like GPT-4. This subchapter delves into the nuanced ethical considerations when using and developing prompts for LLMs, exploring bias, privacy, and responsible AI use. By understanding these challenges, users and developers can create and deploy AI solutions that are both effective and ethically sound.

1. **Addressing Bias in AI:**

Understanding Bias: Bias in AI can stem from various sources, including biased training data, algorithmic biases, and the inherent biases of developers. These biases can lead to unfair or discriminatory outcomes, affecting the credibility and fairness of AI systems.

Examples of Bias:

Gender Bias: If a model is trained on data that reflects gender stereotypes, it may perpetuate these biases in its responses.
Example Prompt: "Describe a day in the life of a nurse."
Biased Response: "She spends her day taking care of patients and assisting doctors."
Revised Prompt: "Describe a day in the life of a nurse, ensuring gender-neutral language."

Cultural Bias: AI may produce content that reflects cultural biases if the training data predominantly represents a specific culture.
Example Prompt: "Write a story about a family dinner."
Biased Response: A narrative that assumes a Western context.
Revised Prompt: "Write a story about a family dinner in various cultural contexts."

Strategies to Mitigate Bias:

Diverse Training Data: Ensure the training data represents a wide range of demographics and perspectives.

Bias Audits: Regularly conduct audits of AI outputs to identify and address biases.

Inclusive Design Practices: Involve diverse teams in the development process to bring multiple perspectives to the table.

2. Ensuring Privacy and Data Security:

Privacy Concerns: With the ability to process vast amounts of data, GPT-4 raises significant privacy concerns. Handling user data responsibly is crucial to protect individual privacy and comply with data protection regulations.

Examples of Privacy Risks:

Data Retention: Storing user interactions without explicit consent can lead to privacy breaches.

Example Prompt: "Provide personalized financial advice based on user data."

Revised Prompt: "Provide general financial advice without using specific user data."

Sensitive Information: The AI might inadvertently generate or request sensitive information.

Example Prompt: "What should I do if I lose my passport?"

Revised Prompt: "What general steps should someone take if they lose their passport?"

Strategies to Protect Privacy:

Anonymization: Ensure all user data is anonymized to protect identities.

Data Minimization: Collect only the data necessary for the task at hand.

Clear Consent: Obtain clear, informed consent from users before collecting or using their data.

3. Promoting Responsible AI Use:

Responsible AI Principles: Responsible AI use involves deploying AI in ways that are ethical, transparent, and aligned with societal values. This includes ensuring AI systems are used for beneficial purposes and avoiding harm.

Examples of Responsible AI Use:

Transparency: Clearly communicate the capabilities and limitations of AI to users.
Example Communication: "GPT-4 can provide general information but should not replace professional advice."

Accountability: Establish clear accountability for AI-generated content.
Example Prompt: "Generate a report on climate change impacts."
Accountability Statement: "This report was generated by AI and should be reviewed by a human expert for accuracy."

Strategies for Responsible AI Use:

Ethical Guidelines: Develop and adhere to ethical guidelines for AI use.
Human Oversight: Ensure human oversight of AI systems, particularly in high-stakes or sensitive areas.
Continuous Monitoring: Regularly monitor AI outputs and impacts to identify and address any ethical concerns.

4. Navigating the Ethical Landscape of Advanced AI:

Complex Ethical Dilemmas: Advanced AI functionalities introduce complex ethical dilemmas that require nuanced understanding and careful consideration.

Examples of Ethical Dilemmas:

Autonomy vs. Control: Balancing AI autonomy with the need for human control and oversight.

Example Scenario: Autonomous AI in healthcare making treatment recommendations.

Ethical Approach: Ensure that final decisions remain with human healthcare professionals.

Innovation vs. Regulation: Encouraging AI innovation while ensuring it is regulated to prevent misuse.

Example Scenario: Developing new AI applications in financial services.

Ethical Approach: Work with regulators to ensure innovations comply with ethical standards and regulations.

Strategies for Ethical Navigation:

Ethical Training: Provide ongoing ethical training for AI developers and users.

Stakeholder Engagement: Engage stakeholders, including ethicists, policymakers, and the public, in discussions about AI ethics.

Scenario Planning: Use scenario planning to anticipate and address potential ethical issues.

Case Study: Ethical Use of AI in Healthcare

1. Scenario:
Deploying GPT-4 to provide preliminary medical advice and triage patients.

2. Ethical Considerations:

Bias: Ensure the AI does not favor certain demographics in its recommendations.

Privacy: Protect patient data and ensure confidentiality.

Accountability: Clearly define the role of AI and ensure human oversight.

3. Implementation:

Prompt Design: "Provide general medical advice based on symptoms while ensuring data privacy and directing users to professional medical services for diagnosis and treatment."

Oversight: Regular review by medical professionals to ensure accuracy and ethical compliance.

By deeply considering these ethical issues and implementing strategies to address them, developers and users of GPT-4 can ensure that AI is used in ways that are not only innovative and effective but also ethically responsible and aligned with societal values. This approach builds trust in AI technologies and ensures they contribute positively to the world.

5.5 Exploring GPT-4's Multimodal Capabilities

G PT-4 is not limited to processing text; it also boasts impressive multimodal capabilities, allowing it to understand and generate text based on image inputs. This section explores how to leverage these capabilities to enhance the scope and depth of AI interactions, offering practical examples and strategies for integrating text and image data effectively.

Understanding Multimodal Capabilities:
Multimodal AI refers to the ability of models like GPT-4 to process and generate content using multiple types of data, such as text, images, and potentially other forms of media. This versatility opens up a range of new applications and enhances existing ones by providing richer context and more detailed responses.

Practical Applications of Multimodal Capabilities:

1. Image Captioning:

Use Case: Automatically generating descriptive captions for images, useful in applications like social media, digital marketing, and accessibility tools.

Example Prompt: "Generate a caption for this image," combined with an image of a sunset over a mountain range.

Enhanced Prompt: "Generate a poetic caption for this image of a sunset over a mountain range, emphasizing the colors and mood of the scene."

2. Visual Question Answering (VQA):

Use Case: Answering questions about the content of an image, useful in educational tools, interactive media, and customer service.

Example Prompt: "What is happening in this image?" with an image showing people playing soccer.

Enhanced Prompt: "Describe the main activities and identify the number of people playing soccer in this image."

3. Content Generation Based on Visual Inputs:

Use Case: Creating stories, articles, or reports based on images, useful for journalism, creative writing, and educational content.

Example Prompt: "Write a short story inspired by this image," with an image of an old, abandoned house.

Enhanced Prompt: "Write a short mystery story inspired by this image of an old, abandoned house, focusing on its history and the secrets it might hold."

4. Interactive Learning Tools:

Use Case: Developing educational materials that combine text and images to enhance learning experiences, useful in e-learning platforms and interactive textbooks.

Example Prompt: "Explain the process shown in this image," with a diagram of the water cycle.

Enhanced Prompt: "Explain the water cycle process shown in this diagram, detailing each step and its significance in the ecosystem."

5. Multimodal Data Analysis:

Use Case: Analyzing and summarizing data that includes both text and visual elements, useful in research, business intelligence, and technical documentation.

Example Prompt: "Summarize the key points from this chart," with an image of a bar chart showing quarterly sales data.

Enhanced Prompt: "Summarize the key points and trends from this bar chart of quarterly sales data, highlighting any significant changes or patterns."

Strategies for Effective Multimodal Prompts:

1. Combining Contextual Information:

Strategy: Provide detailed contextual information in the prompt to guide the AI's interpretation of the image and generation of text.

Example Prompt: "This image shows a historical event. Describe the event and its significance," with an image of the moon landing.

2. Clarifying Desired Output:

Strategy: Clearly specify the type of output you want, whether it's a summary, story, analysis, or description.

Example Prompt: "Analyze the impact of the infrastructure shown in this image on local wildlife," with an image of a highway cutting through a forest.

3. Iterative Refinement:

Strategy: Use iterative prompts to refine the AI's output, providing feedback and requesting additional details or adjustments.

Example Prompt Sequence: Start with "Describe this artwork," then refine with "Explain the use of color and symbolism in this artwork," followed by "Discuss how this artwork reflects the cultural context of its time."

4. Enhancing Engagement:

Strategy: Craft prompts that encourage creative and engaging responses, making use of the AI's ability to generate diverse and imaginative content.

Example Prompt: "Create a travel blog post based on this image of a bustling marketplace," with an image of a lively market scene.

Challenges and Considerations:

1. Accuracy and Relevance:

Challenge: Ensuring the AI's interpretation of the image is accurate and relevant to the prompt.

Solution: Provide clear instructions and context within the prompt to guide the AI's response.

2. Cultural and Contextual Sensitivity:

Challenge: Addressing potential cultural and contextual nuances in images that the AI might misinterpret.

Solution: Include specific cultural or contextual information in the prompt to aid accurate interpretation.

3. Ethical Implications:

Challenge: Avoiding the generation of biased or inappropriate content based on image inputs.

Solution: Implement ethical guidelines and review mechanisms to monitor and refine the AI's outputs.

Future Directions in Multimodal AI:

Enhanced Integration: Future advancements will likely see even more seamless integration of text and visual data, enabling more complex and context-rich interactions.

Broader Applications: As multimodal capabilities improve, we can expect broader applications in fields such as healthcare, where AI could assist in diagnosing conditions based on medical images and patient records.

User Accessibility: Improved multimodal interactions can enhance accessibility tools, providing more comprehensive support for individuals with disabilities.

By exploring and utilizing GPT-4's multimodal capabilities, you can create richer, more engaging, and highly informative AI interactions. Whether for creative projects, educational tools, or business applications, the ability to process and generate text based on image inputs opens up a wide array of possibilities, enhancing the value and impact of AI in various domains.

5.6 Interpreting AI Output

U nderstanding and validating the responses generated by GPT-4 is crucial for ensuring that the AI delivers accurate, relevant, and useful information. This section will discuss techniques for interpreting AI output, evaluating its quality, and making necessary adjustments to enhance its effectiveness.

The Importance of Interpreting AI Output: Interpreting AI output is not just about reading the generated text; it involves assessing its accuracy, relevance, coherence, and alignment with the intended purpose. Proper interpretation ensures that the AI's contributions are valuable and trustworthy.

Techniques for Understanding AI Output:

1. Contextual Analysis:

Technique: Analyze the output within the context of the prompt and the broader conversation. Check if the AI's response aligns with the given context and addresses the prompt accurately.

Example: If the prompt is "Explain the benefits of renewable energy," ensure the response focuses on renewable energy and its benefits, without veering off-topic.

2. Cross-Referencing:

Technique: Validate the AI's response by cross-referencing it with reliable sources. This is particularly important for factual information and technical details.

Example: If GPT-4 generates a response about the latest advancements in AI, verify the details against trusted industry publications or academic papers.

3. Consistency Check:

Technique: Ensure the AI's output is consistent throughout the response and with previous interactions. Inconsistent or contradictory information can undermine the reliability of the content.

Example: In a multi-turn conversation about climate change, check that the AI maintains a consistent viewpoint and uses consistent terminology across responses.

4. Clarity and Coherence:

Technique: Evaluate the clarity and coherence of the AI's output. The response should be logically structured and easy to understand.

Example: For a prompt asking for a summary of a scientific paper, ensure the AI provides a clear, concise, and logically organized summary.

5. Bias Detection:

Technique: Identify and mitigate any biases in the AI's output. This involves being aware of potential biases in the training data and how they might influence the AI's responses.

Example: If the AI generates a response about career advice, check for any gender or cultural biases and adjust the prompt or response to promote fairness.

6. Relevance Assessment:

Technique: Assess the relevance of the AI's response to the prompt. The information provided should be directly related to the query and contribute meaningfully to the conversation.

Example: For a prompt asking for tips on improving mental health, ensure the response stays on topic and provides practical, relevant advice.

7. Sentiment and Tone Analysis:

Technique: Analyze the sentiment and tone of the AI's output to ensure it matches the intended style and emotional impact.

Example: If the prompt requests a motivational message, check that the AI's response is positive and uplifting.

Validating AI Responses:

1. Human Review:

Technique: Have a human reviewer evaluate the AI's responses for accuracy, relevance, and appropriateness. This is especially important for high-stakes or sensitive content.

Example: For medical advice generated by AI, a healthcare professional should review the output to ensure it is accurate and safe.

2. Feedback Loops:

Technique: Implement feedback mechanisms where users can provide input on the AI's responses. Use this feedback to iteratively improve the AI's performance.

Example: After generating customer support responses, collect feedback from users on the helpfulness and clarity of the answers and adjust the prompts accordingly.

3. Automated Validation Tools:

Technique: Utilize automated tools and algorithms to check for factual accuracy, grammatical correctness, and adherence to predefined guidelines.

Example: Use grammar and fact-checking tools to automatically validate content generated by GPT-4 before publishing.

4. Scenario Testing:

Technique: Test the AI's responses across various scenarios to evaluate its robustness and adaptability. This helps identify potential weaknesses and areas for improvement.

Example: Create different scenarios related to emergency response and test how well the AI can generate appropriate guidance for each situation.

5. Ethical Review:

Technique: Conduct an ethical review of the AI's responses to ensure they meet ethical standards and do not propagate harmful stereotypes or misinformation.

Example: Review AI-generated content for cultural sensitivity and inclusiveness, especially in diverse and multicultural contexts.

Case Study: Improving AI Responses in Customer Support

1. Initial Prompt and Response:

Prompt: "How can I reset my password?"

Initial AI Response: "To reset your password, go to the settings page and follow the instructions."

2. Human Review:

Feedback: The response is too generic and does not address potential user issues like forgotten passwords or account recovery options.

Refined Prompt: "Explain the steps to reset a forgotten password and what to do if the user no longer has access to their email."

3. Improved AI Response:

Updated Response: "To reset a forgotten password, go to the login page and click 'Forgot Password.' Enter your email address, and you'll receive a link to reset your password. If you no longer have access to your email, contact our support team for further assistance."

4. Scenario Testing:

Additional Scenario: "What if I can't remember my security questions?"

Refined Prompt: "Include steps for resetting a password when security questions are forgotten."

5. Final AI Response:

Comprehensive Response: "To reset a forgotten password, go to the login page and click 'Forgot Password.' Enter your email address, and you'll receive a link to reset your password. If you can't remember your security questions, select the option to contact our support team for further assistance."

By employing these techniques for interpreting and validating AI output, you can ensure that the responses generated by GPT-4 are accurate, relevant, and trustworthy. This not only enhances the user experience but also builds confidence in the reliability and effectiveness of AI-driven solutions.

Chapter 6:

Practical Applications and Innovations

6.1 Case Studies on GPT-4 Integration

In this section, we explore real-world applications of GPT-4 across various fields. These case studies highlight success stories and lessons learned from early adopters, demonstrating the transformative potential of advanced AI prompts.

Case Study 1: Content Creation

Generating Text Formats:

Application: A digital marketing agency used GPT-4 to generate diverse content formats, including articles, blog posts, product descriptions, social media content, scripts, poems, and musical pieces.

Success Story: The agency reported a 40% increase in content production efficiency, allowing their writers to focus on more strategic tasks.

Lesson Learned: Clear, specific prompts resulted in higher quality and more relevant content. Iterative refinement of prompts based on feedback further improved output quality.

Website Copywriting:

Application: An e-commerce platform integrated GPT-4 to create SEO-optimized content for landing pages and product descriptions.

Success Story: The platform saw a 30% increase in organic traffic and a 20% boost in conversion rates within three months.

Lesson Learned: Incorporating keyword-rich prompts and continuously updating them based on SEO performance metrics led to better search engine rankings and user engagement.

Advertising:

Application: A global advertising firm used GPT-4 to generate headlines, slogans, and ad copy variations.

Success Story: Campaigns using AI-generated copy outperformed traditional ones by 25% in engagement metrics.

Lesson Learned: Testing multiple variations generated by GPT-4 helped identify the most effective messaging, proving the value of A/B testing.

Email Marketing:

Application: An email marketing service provider leveraged GPT-4 to create personalized email content and subject lines.

Success Story: Personalized emails generated by GPT-4 had a 15% higher open rate and a 10% higher click-through rate compared to non-personalized emails.

Lesson Learned: Using customer data to tailor prompts enabled more engaging and relevant email content, enhancing customer interactions.

Case Study 2: Creative Exploration

Image Generation:

Application: An art studio used GPT-4 to generate original artwork based on text prompts, such as "a cyberpunk cityscape."

Success Story: The studio launched a successful NFT collection, with AI-generated artwork selling out within hours.

Lesson Learned: Detailed and imaginative prompts led to more visually striking and marketable artwork. Collaborative refinement between artists and AI enhanced creativity.

Music Generation:

Application: A music production company employed GPT-4 to compose music in various styles and moods.

Success Story: AI-composed pieces were featured in commercials and independent films, broadening the company's portfolio.

Lesson Learned: Specifying musical genres, instruments, and moods in prompts produced compositions that met specific project requirements effectively.

Video Storyboarding:

Application: A video production house used GPT-4 to generate visual concepts for video projects based on text descriptions.

Success Story: The AI-assisted storyboarding process reduced pre-production time by 50%.

Lesson Learned: Providing clear narrative elements and visual themes in prompts resulted in coherent and compelling storyboards.

Game Design:

Application: A game development company integrated GPT-4 to create storylines, quests, and in-game dialogue.

Success Story: AI-generated content enriched the game world, enhancing player engagement and storytelling depth.

Lesson Learned: Iterative collaboration between game designers and GPT-4 ensured that the generated content aligned with the game's vision and narrative style.

Case Study 3: Productivity and Communication

Summarizing Text:

Application: A research organization used GPT-4 to create concise summaries of articles, reports, and emails.

Success Story: Researchers saved significant time, allowing them to focus more on analysis and experimentation.

Lesson Learned: Prompts specifying desired summary length and focus areas led to more relevant and useful summaries.

Translating Languages:

Application: A translation service integrated GPT-4 to aid in human translation efforts and generate rough translations.

Success Story: The service improved translation turnaround times and expanded its language offerings.

Lesson Learned: Including context and target audience details in prompts improved translation accuracy and relevance.

Writing Different Styles:

Application: A corporate communications team used GPT-4 to draft formal reports, casual emails, and creative writing pieces.

Success Story: The team reported increased productivity and enhanced writing quality.

Lesson Learned: Tailoring prompts to specify the tone and style needed for each document type yielded the best results.

Brainstorming Ideas:

Application: An innovation consultancy utilized GPT-4 to generate creative concepts and solutions based on keywords.

Success Story: The AI-assisted brainstorming sessions led to breakthrough ideas for client projects.

Lesson Learned: Combining human expertise with AI-generated ideas in brainstorming sessions maximized creativity and practicality.

Case Study 4: Research and Development

Scientific Paper Writing:

Application: A biotech company used GPT-4 to automate the writing of introductions, methods, and results sections of scientific papers.

Success Story: Researchers could focus more on experimental design and data analysis, improving overall productivity.

Lesson Learned: Detailed prompts including specific scientific jargon and structured formats produced high-quality academic writing.

Drug Discovery:

Application: A pharmaceutical firm employed GPT-4 to analyze data and identify promising drug candidates.

Success Story: The firm accelerated its drug discovery process, identifying several potential candidates for further testing.

Lesson Learned: Combining AI analysis with human expertise in interpreting results led to more accurate and actionable insights.

Climate Research:

Application: An environmental research group used GPT-4 to simulate future climate scenarios based on existing data.

Success Story: The AI-assisted simulations provided valuable insights for policy recommendations.

Lesson Learned: Incorporating comprehensive datasets and specifying scenario parameters in prompts enhanced the accuracy and relevance of simulations.

Data Analysis:

Application: A data analytics company integrated GPT-4 to generate reports and summaries of large datasets.

Success Story: The company improved its reporting efficiency and quality, delivering better insights to clients.

Lesson Learned: Detailed prompts that included specific analysis goals and key metrics produced the most relevant and insightful reports.

Case Study 5: Software Development

Writing Code:

Application: A software development firm used GPT-4 to generate code snippets for specific functionalities.

Success Story: The firm accelerated its development process, reducing time-to-market for new features.

Lesson Learned: Clear and precise prompts specifying the programming language and functionality needed resulted in accurate and usable code snippets.

Testing Software:

Application: A quality assurance team employed GPT-4 to create automated test cases based on software functionalities.

Success Story: The team improved its testing coverage and efficiency, identifying more bugs before release.

Lesson Learned: Detailed prompts describing the software functionality and expected outcomes led to more effective and comprehensive test cases.

Case Study 6: Education and Learning

Personalized Learning:

Application: An educational technology company used GPT-4 to generate practice materials tailored to individual student needs.

Success Story: Students reported higher engagement and improved learning outcomes with personalized materials.

Lesson Learned: Including specific learning objectives and student performance data in prompts produced more relevant and effective practice materials.

Language Learning:

Application: A language learning app integrated GPT-4 to create conversational prompts and exercises for language practice.

Success Story: Users experienced faster language acquisition and greater enjoyment in learning.

Lesson Learned: Contextual and culturally relevant prompts enhanced the realism and effectiveness of language practice exercises.

These case studies illustrate the diverse applications and transformative potential of GPT-4 across various fields. By leveraging advanced AI prompts, early adopters have achieved significant improvements in efficiency, creativity, and productivity, offering valuable lessons for future implementations.

6.2 Exploring AI Integrations with IoT

The integration of AI with the Internet of Things (IoT) represents a significant advancement in technology, combining the predictive and analytical capabilities of AI with the vast network of interconnected devices that characterize IoT. This section will explore how AI prompts can enhance IoT applications, discussing various use cases and the benefits of these integrations.

Introduction to AI and IoT Integration:

AI and IoT integration involves using AI algorithms to analyze and interpret the vast amounts of data generated by IoT devices. This synergy can lead to smarter, more responsive systems that can predict issues before they arise, optimize performance, and provide deeper insights into operations.

Use Cases for AI Prompts in IoT:

Smart Homes:

Application: AI can analyze data from various smart home devices (thermostats, lights, security cameras) to enhance user convenience and security.

Example Prompt: "Analyze the energy usage data from the past month and suggest optimizations to reduce electricity bills."

Outcome: AI analyzes patterns in energy consumption and recommends changes, such as adjusting thermostat settings or scheduling appliances to run during off-peak hours.

Predictive Maintenance:

Application: In industrial IoT, AI can predict when machinery will need maintenance, preventing costly downtime.

Example Prompt: "Monitor the vibration data from the manufacturing equipment and predict any maintenance needs."

Outcome: AI predicts potential failures by analyzing sensor data, allowing maintenance teams to address issues proactively.

Healthcare Monitoring:

Application: AI can process data from wearable devices and smart health monitors to track patient health and predict medical issues.

Example Prompt: "Analyze heart rate and activity data to identify patterns that may indicate a health issue."

Outcome: AI detects anomalies in the data that could signal a health problem, prompting early intervention by healthcare providers.

Agricultural Optimization:

Application: AI can optimize farming operations by analyzing data from soil sensors, weather stations, and drones.

Example Prompt: "Analyze soil moisture and weather data to recommend the best times for irrigation."

Outcome: AI provides precise irrigation schedules that conserve water and improve crop yields.

Smart Cities:

Application: AI can enhance the management of city infrastructure, including traffic flow, waste management, and energy distribution.
Example Prompt: "Analyze traffic patterns to suggest improvements in signal timings for reducing congestion."
Outcome: AI optimizes traffic light timings, reducing congestion and improving traffic flow.

Benefits of AI and IoT Integration:

Enhanced Efficiency:

Benefit: AI-driven insights lead to more efficient use of resources and streamlined operations.
Example: In smart buildings, AI can optimize heating, ventilation, and air conditioning (HVAC) systems based on occupancy data, reducing energy consumption.

Predictive Capabilities:

Benefit: AI's ability to predict future events based on historical data helps prevent issues and optimize maintenance schedules.
Example: In predictive maintenance, AI can forecast equipment failures, allowing timely interventions that prevent costly breakdowns.

Improved Decision-Making:

Benefit: AI provides actionable insights that aid in making informed decisions quickly.
Example: In agriculture, AI can analyze environmental data to provide farmers with recommendations that enhance crop management.

Personalization:

Benefit: AI enables personalized experiences by adapting to individual preferences and behaviors.

Example: In smart homes, AI can learn the preferences of occupants and adjust lighting, temperature, and other settings automatically.

Scalability:

Benefit: AI systems can easily scale to handle large volumes of data from numerous IoT devices.

Example: In smart cities, AI can manage and analyze data from thousands of sensors to optimize urban infrastructure and services.

Challenges and Considerations:

Data Privacy and Security:

Challenge: Protecting sensitive data collected by IoT devices from breaches and misuse.

Consideration: Implement robust encryption and access control measures to safeguard data.

Interoperability:

Challenge: Ensuring that different IoT devices and systems can communicate and work together seamlessly.

Consideration: Adopt standardized protocols and interfaces to facilitate interoperability.

Data Quality:

Challenge: Ensuring the accuracy and reliability of data from IoT devices.

Consideration: Regularly calibrate and maintain IoT devices to ensure data quality.

Scalability:

Challenge: Managing the increasing volume of data generated by IoT devices as systems scale up.

Consideration: Use scalable cloud-based solutions and efficient data processing algorithms.

Ethical Considerations:

Challenge: Addressing ethical issues related to AI decision-making and its impact on society.

Consideration: Develop ethical guidelines and frameworks to govern AI use in IoT applications.

Future Directions:

Edge AI:

Development: Implementing AI processing at the edge, closer to where data is generated, to reduce latency and improve real-time decision-making.

Example: Using edge AI in autonomous vehicles to process sensor data locally for faster response times.

Enhanced AI Algorithms:

Development: Developing more sophisticated AI algorithms that can handle complex IoT data and provide deeper insights.

Example: Advanced machine learning models that can predict multiple variables simultaneously in smart city management.

Integration with 5G:

Development: Leveraging 5G networks to enhance the connectivity and data transfer capabilities of IoT devices.

Example: Using 5G to enable real-time communication between medical devices and AI systems in healthcare.

Sustainable IoT:

Development: Focusing on sustainable practices in IoT deployments to reduce environmental impact.

Example: Using AI to optimize energy use in smart grids, contributing to greener cities.

By integrating AI with IoT, we unlock new possibilities for efficiency, innovation, and personalization across various industries. As these technologies continue to evolve, the synergy between AI and IoT will drive significant advancements, making our environments smarter, more responsive, and more sustainable.

Chapter 7

Conclusion

7.1 The Journey Ahead: Continuing Your AI Exploration

So, you've made it through the guide, and your journey with AI prompt crafting is just beginning. Pretty exciting, right? In this section, we'll share some handy tips and resources to keep you learning, exploring, and mastering the art of prompt crafting. Whether you're just starting out or already pretty advanced, there's always something new to discover. Let's get into it!

Staying Updated with Prompt Crafting Techniques:

AI and prompt crafting are fields that are always evolving. Keeping up with the latest techniques can help you stay ahead of the curve.

Follow Blogs and Forums: Make it a habit to follow blogs, forums, and communities that focus on AI and prompt crafting. Websites like OpenAI's blog, AI Dungeon community forums, and Reddit's r/PromptCrafting are great places to start. These platforms often share new ideas, best practices, and updates that can be incredibly useful.

Subscribe to Newsletters: Sign up for newsletters from AI research institutions and tech news websites. This way, you can get regular updates on new prompt crafting techniques and best practices delivered straight to your inbox.

Engaging in Online Learning:

Learning doesn't stop after finishing this guide. There are plenty of online resources that can help you dive deeper into the world of AI and prompt crafting.

Advanced Courses: Consider enrolling in advanced courses that focus specifically on prompt engineering and AI interactions. Platforms like

Coursera, Udacity, and edX offer courses that can take your skills to the next level. Look for courses that cover advanced topics and provide hands-on projects.

Workshops and Webinars: Participate in workshops and webinars that focus on the latest developments in prompt crafting and AI applications. These events often feature industry experts who can provide valuable insights and answer your questions.

Experimenting with New Prompts:

One of the best ways to improve is by practicing and experimenting with new prompts. This helps you understand what works and what doesn't, and it can lead to some creative and effective interactions with AI.

Regular Practice: Make a habit of regularly crafting new prompts and experimenting with different styles and formats. Use platforms like OpenAI Playground to test and refine your prompts. The more you practice, the better you'll become at creating effective and engaging prompts.

Challenging Scenarios: Challenge yourself with new and complex scenarios. Push the boundaries of what you can achieve with GPT-4 by creating prompts for various applications, such as storytelling, data analysis, customer service, and more. This will help you develop a versatile skill set.

Leveraging GPT-4's Browsing Capabilities:

Remember, GPT-4 can now browse the internet to fetch current information. This feature can be incredibly powerful for creating up-to-date and relevant prompts.

Current Information: Craft prompts that ask GPT-4 to fetch and summarize the latest research, news, or trends in your area of interest. This ensures that your interactions are always relevant and based on the most recent information available.

Example: "Fetch the latest research on renewable energy trends in 2024 and summarize the key findings."

Building an Advanced Prompt Portfolio:

Creating a collection of your best prompts can be a valuable practice. It helps you track your progress, refine your techniques, and showcase your skills.

Organize Your Prompts: Start by organizing your prompts by use case, complexity, and effectiveness. Use tags and annotations to highlight key features and outcomes. This makes it easier to find and reuse prompts when needed.

Digital Portfolio: Create a digital portfolio using platforms like GitHub, Google Drive, or a personal website. Regularly update it with new and refined prompts. This portfolio can serve as a personal reference or be shared with others in your professional network.

Share and Receive Feedback: Share your prompt portfolio with peers, mentors, and the AI community to receive constructive feedback and suggestions. Participating in prompt crafting competitions and challenges can also be a great way to test your skills and gain recognition for your work.

By staying engaged and continuously improving your prompt crafting skills, you can unlock the full potential of GPT-4 and future AI models. Remember, the journey doesn't end here—it's an ongoing adventure of learning, experimenting, and refining your abilities. Keep exploring, stay curious, and most importantly, have fun with it!

7.2 Keeping Up with Advanced Prompt Crafting: Navigating the Continuous Evolution

AI and prompt crafting are fields that evolve at lightning speed. Keeping up with the latest advancements and trends is essential to stay ahead and make the most of these incredible technologies. In this section, we'll dive into how you can stay updated with the continuous evolution of advanced prompt crafting and ensure your skills remain sharp and relevant.

Following Industry Leaders and Publications:

One of the best ways to stay informed about the latest in AI and prompt crafting is to follow industry leaders and publications. These sources often provide insights into cutting-edge research, new techniques, and emerging trends.

Tip: Follow AI researchers, prompt engineers, and industry leaders on social media platforms like Twitter and LinkedIn. These platforms are goldmines for up-to-date information and direct insights from experts.

Resource: Subscribe to publications and research papers from leading AI conferences such as NeurIPS, ICML, and AAAI. These conferences showcase the latest breakthroughs and innovative approaches in AI and prompt crafting.

Utilizing GPT-4's Browsing Capabilities:

With GPT-4's ability to browse the internet, you have a powerful tool at your disposal to access the latest information. This capability allows you to create prompts that incorporate current data and insights.

Tip: Leverage GPT-4's browsing feature to fetch real-time information on AI developments, market trends, and recent research. This ensures your prompts are always relevant and up-to-date.

Example Prompt: "Fetch the latest advancements in natural language processing research and summarize the key findings."

Engaging in Continuous Learning:

The field of AI is dynamic, and continuous learning is crucial to keep up with its rapid evolution. Engaging in ongoing education helps you stay current with new tools, techniques, and best practices.

Advanced Courses: Enroll in advanced courses and certifications that focus on AI, machine learning, and prompt engineering. Platforms like Coursera, edX, and Udacity offer specialized courses that can deepen your expertise.

Workshops and Webinars: Participate in workshops, webinars, and online bootcamps that focus on the latest developments in AI and prompt crafting. These events often feature industry experts who provide valuable insights and practical advice.

Participating in AI Communities and Forums:

Engaging with AI communities and forums allows you to learn from others, share your experiences, and stay updated on the latest trends.

Tip: Join AI-focused communities on platforms like Reddit (r/MachineLearning, r/PromptCrafting), Stack Overflow, and specialized LinkedIn groups. These communities are great places to ask questions, share your work, and get feedback.

Activity: Participate in discussions, contribute your insights, and collaborate on projects. This interaction helps you stay connected with peers and experts in the field.

Attending AI Conferences and Meetups:

Conferences and meetups offer excellent opportunities to network with professionals, learn about the latest research, and gain insights from industry leaders.

Tip: Attend major AI conferences such as NeurIPS, ICML, AAAI, and AI Expo. Many of these conferences offer virtual attendance options, making it easier to participate from anywhere.

Activity: Engage in conference sessions, workshops, and networking events. These interactions can provide valuable knowledge and foster professional connections.

Reading AI Research Papers:

Staying informed about the latest research is essential for advanced prompt crafting. Reading AI research papers helps you understand new methodologies, applications, and theoretical advancements.

Tip: Use platforms like arXiv, Google Scholar, and ResearchGate to access AI research papers. Set aside regular time to read and digest new research.

Activity: Summarize key takeaways from the papers you read and consider how these insights can be applied to your prompt crafting techniques.

Implementing Ethical and Responsible AI Practices:

As AI evolves, so do the ethical considerations. It's crucial to stay informed about ethical guidelines and best practices to ensure responsible use of AI.

Tip: Study AI ethics, fairness, and transparency through resources like the AI Ethics Guidelines from the European Commission or the Partnership on AI.

Activity: Incorporate ethical considerations into your prompt crafting practices. Ensure your prompts promote fairness, avoid bias, and respect user privacy.

Exploring New AI Tools and Platforms:

New AI tools and platforms are continually being developed, offering enhanced capabilities and new features. Exploring these tools can keep your skills relevant and open up new possibilities.

Tip: Stay updated on the latest AI tools and platforms by following tech news websites and AI tool repositories like GitHub.

Activity: Experiment with new tools and integrate them into your prompt crafting process. This hands-on experience helps you stay adaptable and innovative.

Collaborating with Peers and Experts:

Collaboration can spark new ideas and provide fresh perspectives. Working with others can help you learn new techniques and refine your skills.

Tip: Collaborate on projects with peers, join study groups, or seek mentorship from experienced AI professionals.

Activity: Engage in collaborative projects, participate in hackathons, and seek feedback on your work. These activities foster continuous learning and improvement.

By embracing these strategies, you can navigate the continuous evolution of advanced prompt crafting and maintain a cutting-edge skill set. Staying updated, engaging in lifelong learning, and leveraging new tools and techniques will ensure you remain a proficient and innovative prompt crafter in the ever-changing landscape of AI. Keep exploring, stay curious, and continue to unlock the power of advanced prompts!

7.3 Future Directions with GPT-4 and Beyond

You've truly mastered the craft of prompt crafting with GPT-4, but remember, the AI landscape is always evolving. The future promises even more revolutionary developments in AI technologies and prompt crafting capabilities. In this section, we'll delve into potential future directions for GPT-4 and subsequent models, providing insights on how to stay prepared and proactive in embracing these advancements. Let's explore what lies ahead and how you can gear up for these exhilarating innovations!

Anticipating New Features and Capabilities:

As AI technology progresses, expect to see new features and enhanced capabilities in upcoming models. Being well-informed about these changes is crucial for leveraging the most advanced tools and techniques in prompt crafting.

Tip: Regularly check updates from leading AI research organizations like OpenAI, DeepMind, and Google AI. They are often at the forefront of breakthroughs in AI technologies.

Resource: Participate in beta programs or early access trials when available. Early adoption can provide a significant advantage in understanding and utilizing new features effectively.

Enhanced Contextual Understanding:

Future AI models are expected to achieve even greater heights in contextual understanding, enabling them to generate responses that are not only accurate but also deeply nuanced.

Example: Envision an AI that seamlessly remembers and builds upon previous interactions, capable of sustaining extended conversations with coherence. This capability will be invaluable for complex applications such as in-depth research and comprehensive project management.

Expanding Multimodal Capabilities:

The integration of multimodal capabilities will allow future AI to engage with multiple types of data — text, images, audio — creating richer and more interactive experiences.

Tip: Start familiarizing yourself with simple multimodal tasks, like generating captions for images or summarizing audio content.

Example Prompt: "Create a visual and textual analysis of the latest trends in digital art."

Advanced Personalization and Adaptive Learning:

Look forward to AI models that offer sophisticated personalization and adaptive learning features, tailoring responses based on individual user preferences and continually improving from past interactions.

Tip: Begin experimenting with current personalization features and provide feedback to influence future developments.

Example Prompt: "Develop a customized learning module based on my past interactions, focusing on advanced prompt crafting techniques."

Integration with Internet of Things (IoT):

As AI becomes more integrated with IoT devices, anticipate more seamless interactions between AI and everyday environments, potentially transforming homes, workplaces, and public spaces into smarter ecosystems.

Tip: Explore practical applications of AI in managing and optimizing IoT devices in your environment.

Example Prompt: "Optimize the energy management in my smart home based on usage patterns collected over the past month."

Ethical and Responsible AI Development:

The importance of ethical considerations in AI development will continue to grow, with future directions likely emphasizing the creation of robust frameworks to ensure fairness and transparency.

Tip: Stay informed and actively participate in discussions around AI ethics to ensure your prompt crafting practices are responsible.

Activity: Implement guidelines in your work to ensure that your AI interactions are ethically sound and socially responsible.

Collaborative AI Systems:

Expect advancements in AI systems that can collaborate among themselves to solve complex problems, potentially leading to a new era of cooperative intelligence.

Tip: Start exploring how different AI models can be integrated to enhance problem-solving capabilities.

Example Prompt: "Collaborate with an AI specializing in economic forecasts to enhance the market analysis report."

Specialization in AI for Diverse Industries:

AI models will become increasingly specialized, fine-tuned for specific sectors such as healthcare, finance, and education, enhancing their effectiveness and applicability in these fields.

Tip: Identify opportunities in your industry where specialized AI applications could be revolutionary.

Example Prompt: "Generate a report on the latest AI-driven innovations in personalized medicine."

Embracing Continuous Learning and Improvement:

Future AI models will likely excel in learning continuously, updating their knowledge base in real-time without extensive retraining—a feature that will be essential for staying current in fast-evolving fields.

Tip: Adopt a mindset of continuous learning, staying curious, and regularly updating your skills and knowledge.

Activity: Regularly revise and update your prompts to reflect the latest information and AI capabilities.

Preparing for an AI-Driven Future:

To stay ahead in the rapidly advancing world of AI, proactive preparation and a willingness to adapt are essential.

Stay Informed: Keep abreast of the latest research, trends, and news in AI to ensure you are always ahead of the curve.

Experiment Boldly: Continuously push the boundaries with new prompts and AI features to explore the full potential of what AI can achieve.

Engage Actively: Participate in AI communities, share your experiences, and collaborate on innovative projects to enhance your knowledge and skills.

Invest in Learning: Consider further education such as advanced courses and certifications to deepen your understanding and expertise in the field.

By preparing for these future directions and embracing the continuous evolution of AI and advanced prompt crafting, you ensure that you remain at the cutting edge of technology. Stay enthusiastic, keep exploring, and get ready to unlock the immense potential of GPT-4 and beyond. The future is bright, and with the right tools and knowledge, you'll be well-equipped to meet it head-on. Exciting times are indeed ahead, and the journey continues!

7.4 Building an AI Prompt Portfolio

As you continue to refine your skills in working with GPT-4 and other advanced AI tools, it's essential to develop a comprehensive portfolio of your best prompts. This portfolio not only showcases your ability to effectively communicate with AI but also serves as a practical resource you can refer to when facing new challenges or sharing your expertise with others. Let's walk through how to build and maintain an advanced prompt portfolio that highlights your expertise and creativity.

Why Build a Prompt Portfolio?

A prompt portfolio is more than just a collection of your past work; it's a demonstration of your ability to craft precise, nuanced, and effective prompts that elicit the best responses from AI. It provides tangible proof of your prompt crafting skills and helps you:

Reflect on your growth: Tracking your progress over time can be incredibly rewarding and informative.

Share your knowledge: A well-organized portfolio can be a valuable tool for mentoring others or collaborating with peers.

Market your skills: Whether you're seeking employment or freelance opportunities, a robust portfolio showcases your abilities to potential employers or clients.

Starting Your Portfolio:

Begin by selecting a platform or tool where you can easily organize and update your work. Digital formats are particularly useful because they allow for easy editing and sharing.

Digital Tools: Consider using platforms like GitHub for a more technical display, or create a visually appealing portfolio with tools like Behance or a personal website.

Organizational Structure: Categorize your prompts by theme, industry, complexity, or effectiveness. This helps viewers navigate your portfolio and quickly find prompts that interest them.

What to Include in Your Portfolio:

Your portfolio should be a curated collection of your work. Choose prompts that showcase a range of skills and outcomes.

Diverse Prompts: Include a variety of prompts that show your range in handling different tasks, from simple informational queries to complex problem-solving.

Success Stories: Highlight prompts that led to particularly successful AI interactions. Include a brief overview of the challenge, your prompt, and the AI's response.

Feedback and Iterations: Show how you've refined prompts based on feedback or further insight, which demonstrates your ability to iterate and improve.

Maintaining and Updating Your Portfolio:

Your prompt portfolio is not a static collection; it should evolve as you develop your skills and as new technologies emerge.

Regular Updates: Add new prompts regularly to keep your portfolio current and relevant.

Reflect on Feedback: Incorporate feedback from peers or mentors to improve the presentation and content of your portfolio.

Stay Current: As AI technologies and capabilities advance, revisit your older prompts to see if they can be improved or need to be retired.

Sharing Your Portfolio:

Once you have built your portfolio, sharing it can help you connect with other AI enthusiasts, potential employers, or collaborators.

Social Media: Use LinkedIn, Twitter, and other social media platforms to share updates or featured prompts from your portfolio.

Blogs and Articles: Write about your process and learnings in crafting prompts. Include links to your portfolio to drive engagement.

Networking Events: Present your portfolio at AI meetups, conferences, or workshops. This can be a great way to get feedback and make professional connections.

Utilizing Your Portfolio for Growth:

Beyond showcasing your work, use your portfolio as a tool for continual learning and professional development.

Self-Review: Periodically review your portfolio to assess your growth and identify areas for further learning or development.

Mentorship Opportunities: Use your portfolio as a teaching tool when mentoring others interested in AI and prompt crafting.

Collaborative Projects: Leverage your portfolio to find or create opportunities for collaboration on AI projects that can challenge your skills and lead to new learning experiences.

Building and maintaining an advanced prompt portfolio is a dynamic process that enhances your credibility and showcases your expertise in the field of AI and prompt crafting. It's a testament to your dedication and passion for engaging with cutting-edge technology. So, start compiling your best work today, and keep refining it as you grow. Your portfolio will not only reflect your past achievements but also open doors to future opportunities.

Chapter 8:

Bonus AI Unleashed: 20 Key Applications and Expert Strategies for Success

8.1 Writing Different Kinds of Creative Content

Creative content generation is one of the most fascinating applications of GPT-4. Whether it's writing short stories, poems, or scripts, AI can significantly enhance creativity by providing fresh ideas and perspectives. This section will explore how to craft effective prompts for various types of creative content, leveraging GPT-4's capabilities to inspire and generate innovative outputs.

Example Prompts:

1. **Short Story Creation:**

Prompt: "Write a short story about a detective who solves a mystery in an enchanted forest, where the trees whisper secrets and mythical creatures play tricks."

Why it Works: This prompt provides a specific setting and plot elements, guiding the AI to generate a coherent and engaging narrative. It can be adapted by changing the setting or the nature of the mystery.

2. **Poetry Writing:**

Prompt: "Compose a poem about the transition from winter to spring, focusing on the renewal of nature and the gradual return of warmth and light."

Why it Works: The prompt specifies the theme and tone, encouraging the AI to create evocative and imagery-rich poetry. It can be adapted by choosing different seasons or themes.

3. Script Writing for a Commercial (Internet-Connected):

Prompt: "Write a 30-second script for a commercial promoting the latest eco-friendly smartphone. Highlight its sustainable materials, advanced features, and positive impact on the environment. Include the latest statistics on smartphone recycling rates."

Why it Works: The prompt provides clear guidelines for the content and purpose of the commercial, while internet connectivity allows the AI to incorporate up-to-date statistics and information.

4. Interactive Fiction:

Prompt: "Develop an interactive fiction story where the reader makes choices that influence the outcome. Set the story in a dystopian future where society is controlled by a powerful AI. Include at least three decision points that significantly alter the plot."

Why it Works: This prompt outlines the structure and setting for the interactive fiction, guiding the AI to create a branching narrative. It can be adapted by changing the setting or the nature of the decisions.

5. Song Lyrics Writing (Internet-Connected):

Prompt: "Write lyrics for a pop song about overcoming challenges and achieving personal growth. Include references to recent motivational quotes from public figures and current trending topics in self-improvement."

Why it Works: The prompt specifies the theme and format, while the internet connectivity allows the AI to include contemporary references, making the lyrics relevant and inspiring.

Conclusion: Using GPT-4 for creative content generation can unlock new levels of creativity and productivity. By crafting specific and imaginative prompts, you can guide the AI to produce high-quality stories, poems, scripts, and more. Remember to adapt prompts based on your needs and take advantage of the AI's internet connectivity to include up-to-date information and trends. This approach ensures that your creative content is both innovative and relevant.

8.2 Answering Your Questions in an Informative Way

One of the most powerful applications of GPT-4 is its ability to provide detailed, informative responses to a wide range of questions. By crafting well-structured prompts, you can leverage the AI's extensive knowledge base and, with its internet connectivity, access the latest information to answer questions comprehensively. This section will explore how to create effective prompts for generating informative answers.

Example Prompts:

1. **Explaining Complex Concepts:**

Prompt: "Explain the process of photosynthesis in simple terms suitable for a 10-year-old. Include the role of sunlight, water, and carbon dioxide in the process."

Why it Works: The prompt specifies the target audience and the key elements of the process, ensuring the AI provides a clear and age-appropriate explanation. It can be adapted for different age groups or scientific processes.

2. Comparing Technologies (Internet-Connected):

Prompt: "Compare the advantages and disadvantages of 5G and 4G networks. Include recent developments and statistics from the past year."

Why it Works: The prompt asks for a comparison and specifies that the information should be current, utilizing the AI's internet connectivity to provide the latest data and insights.

3. Historical Analysis:

Prompt: "Describe the key factors that led to the fall of the Roman Empire. Focus on economic, military, and political reasons."

Why it Works: The prompt outlines the specific aspects to be covered, guiding the AI to provide a comprehensive analysis of the historical event. It can be adapted by changing the historical event or factors to be analyzed.

4. Health and Wellness Advice (Internet-Connected):

Prompt: "Provide a summary of the latest research on the benefits of intermittent fasting. Include findings from studies published in the last two years."

Why it Works: This prompt directs the AI to provide up-to-date health information, leveraging its internet connectivity to access the most recent studies and findings.

5. Understanding Current Events:

Prompt: "Explain the causes and implications of the recent economic downturn. Focus on key factors such as unemployment rates, inflation, and government policies."

Why it Works: The prompt specifies the key factors to be discussed, ensuring the AI provides a thorough and relevant analysis of the current event. It can be adapted for different economic events or factors.

Conclusion: By crafting precise and well-structured prompts, you can effectively utilize GPT-4's capabilities to answer questions in an informative way. Whether explaining complex concepts, comparing technologies, analyzing historical events, or providing the latest health advice, leveraging both the AI's extensive knowledge base and its internet connectivity ensures comprehensive and up-to-date responses. This approach enhances your ability to obtain detailed and relevant information across various domains.

8.3 Translating Languages: AI as a Multilingual Translator

GPT-4's ability to translate languages accurately and fluently makes it an invaluable tool for breaking down language barriers. Whether you need translations for business communications, travel, or creative projects, crafting effective prompts can help you utilize GPT-4 as a multilingual translator. This section explores how to create prompts for different translation needs, leveraging the AI's internet connectivity for the most accurate and culturally relevant translations.

Example Prompts:

1. Business Communication:

Prompt: "Translate the following email from English to French, ensuring it maintains a professional tone: 'Dear Mr. Dupont, I am writing to discuss our upcoming project and would like to schedule a meeting next week. Please let me know your availability. Best regards, John Smith.'"

Why it Works: This prompt specifies the source and target languages, the tone, and the content to be translated, ensuring a precise and contextually appropriate translation. It can be adapted for different types of business communications and languages.

2. Travel Phrases (Internet-Connected):

Prompt: "Translate these common travel phrases from English to Spanish and include phonetic pronunciations: 'Where is the nearest hotel?', 'How much does this cost?', 'Can you recommend a good restaurant?'"

Why it Works: This prompt provides specific phrases and asks for phonetic pronunciations, making it useful for travelers. Internet connectivity allows the AI to provide accurate and culturally relevant translations.

3. Creative Writing:

Prompt: "Translate this short story from English to Japanese, maintaining the original tone and style: 'Once upon a time, in a small village, there lived a wise old man who could talk to animals. His wisdom was sought by people from far and wide.'"

Why it Works: The prompt specifies the content, tone, and style, guiding the AI to produce a translation that preserves the original story's nuances. It can be adapted for different creative content and languages.

4. Multilingual Customer Support (Internet-Connected):

Prompt: "Translate this customer service response from English to German and ensure it addresses common queries accurately: 'Thank you for contacting us. Your order has been processed and will be shipped within 3-5 business days. If you have any further questions, please feel free to reach out.'"

Why it Works: This prompt provides a specific context and content, ensuring the AI generates an accurate and contextually appropriate translation. Internet connectivity allows for real-time updates and accuracy.

5. Cultural Content Translation:

Prompt: "Translate this cultural essay from English to Italian, ensuring that idiomatic expressions and cultural references are accurately conveyed: 'Italian cuisine is not just about pizza and pasta; it's a reflection of the country's rich history and diverse regions.'"

Why it Works: This prompt specifies the need for accurate translation of idiomatic expressions and cultural references, guiding the AI to produce a translation that resonates with the target audience. It can be adapted for different types of cultural content.

Conclusion: By crafting detailed and context-specific prompts, you can effectively use GPT-4 for accurate and culturally relevant translations. Whether for business communications, travel, creative writing, customer support, or cultural content, leveraging both the AI's linguistic capabilities and its internet connectivity ensures high-quality translations. This approach enhances your ability to communicate across languages and cultures, making GPT-4 an indispensable tool for multilingual interactions.

8.4 Summarizing Factual Topics

Summarizing factual topics is a key strength of GPT-4, allowing users to condense large volumes of information into concise, clear, and informative summaries. This can be particularly useful for quickly understanding complex subjects, reviewing lengthy documents, or creating overviews for presentations. In this section, we'll explore how to craft effective prompts for generating summaries of factual topics, utilizing GPT-4's ability to access and synthesize information.

Example Prompts:

1. Scientific Research Summary:

Prompt: "Summarize the key findings of the latest research on climate change impacts on polar bear populations, including changes in their habitat and food sources."

Why it Works: This prompt is specific about the topic and what details to include, guiding the AI to provide a focused and informative summary. It can be adapted to summarize different research topics.

2. Historical Event Overview:

Prompt: "Provide a summary of the key events and outcomes of the Industrial Revolution, focusing on technological advancements and their social impact."

Why it Works: The prompt specifies the aspects of the Industrial Revolution to cover, ensuring a comprehensive and coherent summary. It can be adapted to other historical events.

3. Tech News Update (Internet-Connected):

Prompt: "Summarize the latest developments in artificial intelligence over the past six months, including major breakthroughs and notable applications."

Why it Works: This prompt leverages GPT-4's internet connectivity to access up-to-date information, providing a current and relevant summary of recent AI advancements.

4. Medical Research Summary (Internet-Connected):

Prompt: "Summarize the findings of recent studies on the effectiveness of mRNA vaccines in preventing COVID-19 variants. Include data from the last year."

Why it Works: The prompt asks for a summary of specific research findings, using internet connectivity to ensure the information is recent and accurate.

5. Financial Report Overview:

Prompt: "Provide a summary of the quarterly financial performance of Apple Inc., highlighting key metrics such as revenue, profit, and market trends."

Why it Works: The prompt is specific about the type of information needed, guiding the AI to provide a clear and informative summary of the financial report. It can be adapted to summarize reports from different companies.

Conclusion: Creating detailed and precise prompts is essential for generating accurate and informative summaries of factual topics using GPT-4. Whether summarizing scientific research, historical events, tech news, medical studies, or financial reports, leveraging the AI's capabilities and internet connectivity ensures that the summaries are current and relevant. This approach enhances your ability to quickly understand complex subjects and stay informed about the latest developments across various fields.

8.5 Creating Different Kinds of Creative Text Formats

GPT-4's versatility allows it to generate a wide range of creative text formats, from poetry and stories to scripts and dialogues. This section will guide you on how to craft prompts that encourage the AI to produce various types of creative content, enhancing your projects with unique and imaginative outputs.

Example Prompts:

1. Haiku Creation:

Prompt: "Compose a haiku about the serenity of a winter morning, focusing on the imagery of snow-covered landscapes and stillness."

Why it Works: This prompt specifies the format (haiku) and the theme (winter morning), guiding the AI to create a concise, imagery-rich poem. It can be adapted by changing the theme or season.

2. Commercial Script (Internet-Connected):

Prompt: "Write a 60-second script for a TV commercial promoting an eco-friendly car. Highlight its sustainability features, fuel efficiency, and impact on reducing carbon emissions. Include recent statistics on the benefits of eco-friendly cars."

Why it Works: This prompt provides clear guidelines for the content and purpose of the commercial, while internet connectivity allows the AI to incorporate up-to-date statistics and information.

3. Character Dialogue:

Prompt: "Create a dialogue between two characters: a seasoned detective and a rookie cop. They are discussing the clues they found at a mysterious crime scene in an abandoned warehouse."

Why it Works: The prompt specifies the characters, setting, and context, ensuring the AI generates a coherent and engaging dialogue. It can be adapted by changing the characters or scenario.

4. Song Lyrics (Internet-Connected):

Prompt: "Write lyrics for a pop song about overcoming adversity and finding strength. Include references to recent motivational quotes from public figures and trending topics in self-improvement."

Why it Works: The prompt specifies the theme and format, while the internet connectivity allows the AI to include contemporary references, making the lyrics relevant and inspiring.

5. Fairy Tale:

Prompt: "Write a fairy tale about a young girl who discovers a magical forest hidden behind her grandmother's house. Include elements of mystery, adventure, and lessons about bravery and kindness."

Why it Works: This prompt provides a clear narrative structure and thematic elements, guiding the AI to create a compelling and moral-driven story. It can be adapted by changing the setting or moral lessons.

Conclusion: Using GPT-4 for creating different kinds of creative text formats can greatly enhance your projects by adding unique and imaginative content. By crafting specific and detailed prompts, you can guide the AI to produce high-quality poetry, stories, scripts, dialogues, and lyrics. Leveraging the AI's internet connectivity for up-to-date and relevant content ensures that your creative outputs are both innovative and engaging. This approach allows you to explore various creative formats and enrich your work with diverse and dynamic text.

8.6 Brainstorming Ideas

GPT-4 can be an invaluable tool for brainstorming, helping you generate a wide array of creative and practical ideas. Whether you're looking to develop business concepts, plot lines for a novel, or innovative solutions to problems, crafting the right prompts can unleash the full potential of AI-assisted brainstorming. This section will explore how to create effective prompts for generating diverse ideas, leveraging GPT-4's extensive knowledge and creativity.

Example Prompts:

1. Tech Startup Ideas:

Prompt: "Brainstorm 10 innovative tech startup ideas that address current challenges in remote work and digital collaboration."

Why it Works: The prompt specifies the focus area (remote work and digital collaboration), encouraging the AI to generate

relevant and contemporary business ideas. It can be adapted for different industries or problem areas.

2. Novel Plot Ideas (Internet-Connected):

Prompt: "Generate 5 unique plot ideas for a science fiction novel that incorporates recent advancements in AI and robotics."

Why it Works: This prompt leverages the AI's internet connectivity to incorporate the latest advancements, ensuring that the plot ideas are both innovative and relevant. It can be adapted for different genres or technological trends.

3. Marketing Campaign Concepts:

Prompt: "Create 7 creative marketing campaign concepts for a new line of eco-friendly household products."

Why it Works: The prompt provides a clear context and objective, guiding the AI to generate diverse and creative marketing strategies. It can be adapted by changing the product or campaign goals.

4. Product Development Ideas:

Prompt: "Brainstorm 10 new product ideas for a company specializing in smart home technology. Focus on innovations that enhance convenience and security."

Why it Works: This prompt specifies the industry and focus areas, ensuring that the AI generates relevant and practical product ideas. It can be adapted for different companies or technological areas.

5. Event Planning Concepts (Internet-Connected):

Prompt: "Generate 5 innovative event planning ideas for a virtual tech conference, incorporating the latest trends in online engagement and interactive experiences."

Why it Works: The prompt uses the AI's internet connectivity to stay updated with the latest trends, ensuring that the event planning ideas are contemporary and engaging. It can be adapted for different types of events or industries.

Conclusion: By creating specific and detailed prompts, you can effectively use GPT-4 for brainstorming a wide range of ideas. Whether for business startups, novel plots, marketing campaigns, product development, or event planning, leveraging both the AI's creativity and its access to up-to-date information ensures diverse and innovative ideas. This approach enhances your ability to generate new concepts and solutions, making GPT-4 an essential tool for brainstorming across various domains.

8.7 Debunking Misinformation

In an era where misinformation can spread rapidly, having reliable tools to debunk false claims is crucial. GPT-4 can be used to identify and correct misinformation by providing accurate, evidence-based information. This section will explore how to craft effective prompts for debunking misinformation, leveraging GPT-4's extensive knowledge base and internet connectivity to ensure accuracy and relevance.

Example Prompts:

1. Health Myths:

Prompt: "Debunk the myth that vaccines cause autism with scientific evidence and references to reputable studies."

Why it Works: This prompt specifies the myth to be debunked and requests scientific evidence, guiding the AI to provide accurate and well-supported information. It can be adapted to address different health myths.

2. Climate Change Denial (Internet-Connected):

Prompt: "Provide factual information to counter the claim that climate change is a hoax. Include recent data and findings from credible sources."

Why it Works: The prompt leverages the AI's internet connectivity to provide up-to-date information and credible sources, ensuring that the response is accurate and reliable.

3. Historical Inaccuracies:

Prompt: "Correct the false claim that the Holocaust never happened by providing historical evidence and references from reputable historians."

Why it Works: This prompt specifies the false claim and asks for historical evidence, guiding the AI to produce a well-supported and factual response. It can be adapted to address various historical inaccuracies.

4. Economic Misconceptions (Internet-Connected):

Prompt: "Debunk the misconception that increasing the minimum wage causes widespread unemployment by providing recent economic studies and data."

Why it Works: The prompt uses the AI's internet connectivity to access recent studies and data, ensuring that the information is current and backed by credible sources.

5. Scientific Misunderstandings:

Prompt: "Correct the misunderstanding that GMOs are inherently dangerous to human health by providing scientific evidence and consensus from health organizations."

Why it Works: This prompt requests scientific evidence and consensus, guiding the AI to provide a well-supported and factual response. It can be adapted to address different scientific misunderstandings.

Conclusion: Using GPT-4 to debunk misinformation requires crafting prompts that are clear and specific about the false claims to be addressed and the type of evidence needed. By leveraging both the AI's extensive knowledge base and its internet connectivity, you can ensure that the responses are accurate, up-to-date, and backed by credible sources. This approach enhances your ability to combat misinformation effectively, promoting a more informed and truthful discourse across various topics.

8.8 Writing Different Kinds of Informal Content

GPT-4 excels in generating informal content, which can be used for personal communications, social media posts, blog entries, and more. Informal content typically requires a conversational tone and a relaxed style, making it accessible and engaging. This section will explore how to craft effective prompts for various types of informal content, ensuring the AI produces friendly and relatable outputs.

Example Prompts:

1.   **Friendly Email:**

Prompt: "Write a friendly email inviting a group of friends to a weekend barbecue. Mention the date, time, location, and ask them to bring their favorite dish."

Why it Works: The prompt specifies the purpose of the email and the key details to include, guiding the AI to create a warm and inviting message. It can be adapted for different types of gatherings.

2. **Casual Blog Post (Internet-Connected):**

Prompt: "Write a casual blog post about the benefits of adopting a pet, including recent statistics and heartwarming anecdotes. Keep the tone friendly and encouraging."

Why it Works: This prompt combines a specific topic with a desired tone and internet connectivity to provide current statistics, resulting in an engaging and informative blog post.

3. Social Media Update:

Prompt: "Create a fun and upbeat social media post announcing a flash sale at a local boutique. Mention the discount, duration of the sale, and a call-to-action for followers to visit the store."

Why it Works: The prompt specifies the key elements to include and the tone, ensuring the AI generates a lively and attention-grabbing post. It can be adapted for different promotions or announcements.

4. Personal Story:

Prompt: "Write a personal story about a memorable road trip, focusing on the beautiful scenery, unexpected adventures, and the friends who were part of the journey."

Why it Works: This prompt provides a clear theme and elements to include, guiding the AI to create a relatable and engaging narrative. It can be adapted by changing the type of journey or the focus of the story.

4. Informal Advice Column (Internet-Connected):

Prompt: "Write an informal advice column about dealing with work-from-home fatigue, including recent tips from productivity experts and personal anecdotes."

Why it Works: The prompt combines a specific topic with a relaxed tone and internet connectivity to provide up-to-date advice, resulting in an informative and friendly advice column.

Conclusion: Creating effective prompts for informal content involves specifying the tone, context, and key details to include. By leveraging GPT-4's ability to generate friendly and relatable text, as well as its internet connectivity for current information, you can produce a wide range of engaging informal content. Whether for emails, blog posts, social media updates, personal stories, or advice columns, this approach ensures that the content resonates with the intended audience and maintains a conversational style.

8.9 Refactoring Code

Refactoring code involves restructuring existing code to improve its readability, efficiency, and maintainability without changing its external behavior. GPT-4 can assist in this process by suggesting improvements and optimizations. This section will guide you on how to craft effective prompts for refactoring code, leveraging GPT-4's programming knowledge to enhance your code quality.

Example Prompts:

1. Improving Readability:

Prompt: "Refactor the following Python code to improve its readability by adding comments and using descriptive variable names."

python Code:

```
def calc(a, b):
    return a * b + (a - b)

result = calc(10, 5)
print(result)
```"

Why it Works: The prompt specifies the need for improved readability, guiding the AI to add comments and use clearer variable names. It can be adapted for different programming languages and code snippets.

2. Optimizing Performance (Internet-Connected):

Prompt: "Optimize the following JavaScript code to reduce its execution time and improve performance. Include recent best practices for performance optimization."

javascript code

```javascript
function slowFunction(arr) {
    let result = [];
    for (let i = 0; i < arr.length; i++) {
        for (let j = 0; j < arr.length; j++) {
            if (arr[i] < arr[j]) {
                result.push(arr[i]);
            }
        }
    }
    return result;
}

console.log(slowFunction([5, 3, 8, 1]));
```"

Why it Works: The prompt asks for performance optimization and leverages internet connectivity to incorporate recent best practices, ensuring the AI provides efficient and up-to-date solutions.

3. Enhancing Maintainability:

Prompt: "Refactor the following Java code to enhance its maintainability by modularizing the code and using design patterns where appropriate."

java code

```java
public class Example {
    public static void main(String[] args) {
        int a = 10;
        int b = 5;
        int result = a * b + (a - b);
        System.out.println(result);
    }
}
```"

Why it Works: The prompt focuses on modularization and design patterns, guiding the AI to restructure the code for better maintainability. It can be adapted to different programming contexts and requirements.

4. Code Simplification (Internet-Connected):

Prompt: "Simplify the following Ruby code by removing unnecessary complexity and using more concise syntax. Include the latest Ruby language features for code simplification."

ruby code

```ruby
def complex_method(arr)
    result = []
    arr.each do |a|
      if a % 2 == 0
        result.push(a)
      end
    end
    return result
end

puts complex_method([1, 2, 3, 4, 5])
```"

Why it Works: The prompt asks for code simplification and utilizes internet connectivity to incorporate the latest language features, ensuring the AI provides modern and streamlined solutions.

5. Ensuring Consistency:

Prompt: "Refactor the following PHP code to ensure consistency in coding style and adherence to PHP-FIG standards."

php code

```php
<?php
    function calculate($a, $b) {
        $result = $a * $b + ($a - $b);
        return $result;
    }

    echo calculate(10, 5);
?>
```
```"

**Why it Works:** The prompt specifies the need for consistent coding style and adherence to standards, guiding the AI to produce code that aligns with best practices. It can be adapted for different coding standards and languages.

**Conclusion:** Using GPT-4 for refactoring code involves crafting prompts that specify the desired improvements, whether for readability, performance, maintainability, simplification, or consistency. By leveraging the AI's programming knowledge and internet connectivity, you can enhance your code quality, making it more efficient, readable, and maintainable. This approach ensures that your code adheres to best practices and remains robust and scalable.

## 8.10 Writing Different Kinds of Technical Content

Technical writing requires precision, clarity, and a thorough understanding of the subject matter. GPT-4 can assist in creating a variety of technical content, such as user manuals, technical specifications, reports, and more. This section will explore how to craft effective prompts for generating different types of technical content, ensuring that the output is accurate, informative, and easy to understand.
```

Example Prompts:

1. User Manual:

Prompt: "Write a detailed user manual for a new smart thermostat, including installation instructions, setup procedures, and troubleshooting tips."

Why it Works: This prompt specifies the type of device and the key sections to include, guiding the AI to produce a comprehensive and user-friendly manual. It can be adapted for different devices and products.

2. Technical Specification (Internet-Connected):

Prompt: "Create a technical specification document for a cloud-based storage system, including system architecture, data encryption methods, and scalability features. Use recent standards and best practices."

Why it Works: The prompt outlines the specific areas to cover and leverages internet connectivity to include up-to-date standards and best practices, ensuring the specification is relevant and thorough.

3. Technical Report:

Prompt: "Generate a technical report on the impact of 5G technology on telecommunications, including data on speed improvements, latency reduction, and potential applications in various industries."

Why it Works: This prompt provides a clear focus for the report and specifies the key metrics to include, guiding the AI to produce an informative and well-structured technical report. It can be adapted for different technologies or impacts.

4. Process Documentation (Internet-Connected):
Prompt: "Write a step-by-step process documentation for deploying a web application on AWS, including setting up the environment, deploying the application, and monitoring performance. Include links to recent AWS documentation."

Why it Works: The prompt specifies the process to document and leverages internet connectivity to provide the most current and accurate information, ensuring the documentation is practical and reliable.

5. White Paper:

Prompt: "Create a white paper on the benefits of implementing artificial intelligence in healthcare, focusing on patient outcomes, cost savings, and future potential. Include case studies and statistical data."

Why it Works: This prompt specifies the focus areas and the need for supporting data and case studies, guiding the AI to produce a comprehensive and persuasive white paper. It can be adapted for different industries or technologies.

Conclusion: Using GPT-4 for technical writing involves crafting detailed and specific prompts that outline the type of content needed and the key areas to cover. By leveraging the AI's knowledge and its ability to access up-to-date information, you can generate high-quality technical content that is accurate, informative, and well-structured. Whether you need user manuals, technical specifications, reports, process documentation, or white papers, this approach ensures that your technical writing meets professional standards and effectively communicates complex information.

8.11 Writing Presentations and Outlines

Creating presentations and outlines is an essential skill for effectively communicating ideas, plans, and research. GPT-4 can assist in generating structured and coherent presentations and outlines, saving time and ensuring clarity. This section will guide you on how to craft effective prompts for generating various types of presentations and outlines, leveraging GPT-4's organizational capabilities.

Example Prompts:

1. Business Presentation:

Prompt: "Create an outline for a business presentation on the launch of a new product line, including sections on market analysis, product features, competitive landscape, and marketing strategy."

Why it Works: This prompt specifies the type of presentation and the key sections to include, guiding the AI to produce a well-organized and comprehensive outline. It can be adapted for different business topics or products.

2. Technical Presentation (Internet-Connected):

Prompt: "Generate a PowerPoint presentation on the latest advancements in quantum computing, including slides on key principles, recent breakthroughs, and potential applications. Use recent research and data."

Why it Works: The prompt outlines the structure of the presentation and leverages internet connectivity to include up-to-date information, ensuring the presentation is current and informative.

3. Educational Outline:

Prompt: "Create an outline for a lecture on the history of the Roman Empire, covering major events, influential figures, and societal changes. Include a timeline of key events."

Why it Works: This prompt specifies the topic and the key elements to cover, guiding the AI to produce a detailed and chronological outline. It can be adapted for different historical periods or educational topics.

4. Research Proposal (Internet-Connected):

Prompt: "Generate an outline for a research proposal on the impact of climate change on marine ecosystems. Include sections on background, research questions, methodology, expected outcomes, and references to recent studies."

Why it Works: The prompt provides a clear structure for the research proposal and leverages internet connectivity to include recent studies, ensuring the proposal is well-supported and relevant.

5. Creative Project Presentation:

Prompt: "Create an outline for a presentation on a creative project, such as a short film. Include sections on the storyline, character development, visual style, and production timeline."

Why it Works: This prompt outlines the key aspects of the creative project, guiding the AI to produce a coherent and engaging presentation outline. It can be adapted for different types of creative projects.

Conclusion: Using GPT-4 to create presentations and outlines involves crafting prompts that specify the structure, content, and key elements needed. By leveraging the AI's ability to organize information and access up-to-date data, you can generate high-quality presentations and outlines that are clear, comprehensive, and engaging. Whether for business, technical, educational, research, or creative purposes, this approach ensures that your presentations and outlines effectively communicate your ideas and plans.

8.12 Bug Fixing in Code

Bug fixing is a critical aspect of software development, ensuring that code runs smoothly and performs as expected. GPT-4 can assist in identifying and fixing bugs by analyzing code and providing solutions. This section will guide you on how to craft effective prompts for bug fixing, leveraging GPT-4's programming knowledge and problem-solving capabilities.

Example Prompts:

1. Identifying Syntax Errors:

Prompt: "Identify and fix the syntax errors in the following Python code."

Python Code

```python
def calc(a, b):
    return a * b + (a - b)

result = calc(10, 5)
print(result)
```

Why it Works: This prompt specifies the task and provides the code, guiding the AI to identify and correct syntax errors. It can be adapted for different programming languages.

2. Debugging Logical Errors (Internet-Connected):

Prompt: "Debug the following JavaScript code to correct the logical error causing incorrect calculations. Include an explanation of the issue.

javascript code

```javascript
function calculate(a, b) {
    return a + b * (a - b);
}

console.log(calculate(10, 5));
```

Why it Works: The prompt specifies the type of error and requests an explanation, leveraging the AI's internet connectivity to provide a detailed and accurate solution. It ensures the code functions correctly and the user understands the fix.

3. Fixing Runtime Errors:

Prompt: "Fix the runtime error in the following Java code, which is causing the application to crash."

java code

```java
public class Main {
    public static void main(String[] args) {
        int[] numbers = {1, 2, 3, 4, 5};
        System.out.println(numbers[5]);
    }
}
```

Why it Works: This prompt specifies the type of error and provides the code, guiding the AI to identify and fix the issue causing the crash. It can be adapted for different programming scenarios.

4. Optimizing Code Performance (Internet-Connected):

Prompt: "Identify and fix the performance issues in the following Ruby code to reduce execution time and improve efficiency. Use recent best practices."

Ruby Code

```ruby
def slow_method(arr)
    result = []
    arr.each do |a|
     arr.each do |b|
      result << a if a < b
     end
    end
    result
    end

    puts slow_method([5, 3, 8, 1])
```

Why it Works: The prompt focuses on performance optimization and leverages internet connectivity to incorporate recent best practices, ensuring the AI provides an efficient solution.

5. Fixing Security Vulnerabilities:

Prompt: "Identify and fix the security vulnerabilities in the following PHP code to prevent SQL injection attacks."

php code

```php
<?php
  $username = $_POST['username'];
  $password = $_POST['password'];
  $query = "SELECT * FROM users WHERE username='$username' AND password='$password'";
  $result = mysqli_query($conn, $query);
?>
```

Why it Works: This prompt specifies the type of vulnerability and provides the code, guiding the AI to enhance security and prevent attacks. It can be adapted for different security issues and programming languages.

Conclusion: Using GPT-4 for bug fixing involves crafting detailed prompts that specify the type of error and provide the relevant code. By leveraging the AI's programming knowledge and problem-solving capabilities, you can efficiently identify and fix bugs, ensuring your code runs smoothly and securely. Whether dealing with syntax errors, logical errors, runtime errors, performance issues, or security vulnerabilities, this approach enhances your ability to maintain high-quality code.

8.13 Data Analysis

Data analysis is a crucial task in many fields, from business and healthcare to social sciences and engineering. GPT-4 can assist in generating insights, summarizing data, and providing recommendations based on data sets. This section will guide you on how to craft effective prompts for data analysis, leveraging GPT-4's capabilities to enhance your understanding and utilization of data.

Example Prompts:

1. Summarizing Data Sets:

Prompt: "Analyze the following data set of sales figures for the past year and provide a summary of the key trends, including best-performing products and sales growth over time."

Data:

Product, Month, Sales
    Product A, January, 120
    Product B, January, 90
    Product A, February, 150
    Product B, February, 110
    ...

Why it Works: This prompt specifies the task and provides the data, guiding the AI to identify and summarize key trends. It can be adapted for different types of data sets.

2. Generating Insights (Internet-Connected):

Prompt: "Using the latest market data, analyze the impact of remote work on productivity levels in the tech industry over the past two years. Include relevant statistics and trends."

Why it Works: The prompt leverages GPT-4's internet connectivity to access up-to-date market data, ensuring that the analysis is current and relevant. It guides the AI to generate insights based on the latest information.

3. Providing Recommendations:

Prompt: "Based on the following customer feedback data, provide recommendations for improving product satisfaction. Focus on the most common issues mentioned by customers."

Data:

Feedback ID, Comment
  1, The battery life is too short.
  2, Excellent user interface but needs more features.
  3, Difficult to set up initially.
  ...

Why it Works: This prompt specifies the task and provides the data, guiding the AI to identify common issues and generate actionable recommendations. It can be adapted for different types of feedback or data sets.

4. Trend Analysis (Internet-Connected):

Prompt: "Analyze the latest trends in renewable energy adoption across different countries. Include data on solar, wind, and hydroelectric power usage, and discuss the factors driving these trends."

Why it Works: The prompt leverages internet connectivity to access recent data on renewable energy, ensuring that the analysis is comprehensive and up-to-date. It guides the AI to provide a detailed trend analysis.

5. Predictive Analysis:

Prompt: "Using the following historical sales data, predict the sales figures for the next quarter. Include any relevant factors that might influence the forecast."

Data:

Quarter, Sales
   Q1 2022, 1000
   Q2 2022, 1100
   Q3 2022, 1050
   Q4 2022, 1200

   ...

Why it Works: This prompt specifies the task and provides historical data, guiding the AI to use past trends to predict future sales figures. It can be adapted for different types of predictive analyses.

Conclusion: Creating effective prompts for data analysis involves specifying the task, providing relevant data, and leveraging GPT-4's capabilities to generate insights, summarize information, and provide recommendations. Whether summarizing data sets, generating insights, providing recommendations, analyzing trends, or performing predictive analysis, this approach ensures that your data analysis is thorough, accurate, and actionable. By utilizing GPT-4 for data analysis, you can enhance your ability to understand and utilize data effectively across various fields.

8.14 Generating Different Creative Text Formats

GPT-4's ability to generate creative text formats makes it a valuable tool for writers, marketers, and content creators. Whether you need to create dialogues, descriptive passages, or multimedia scripts, GPT-4 can produce engaging and innovative content. This section will guide you on how to craft effective prompts for generating various creative text formats, leveraging GPT-4's extensive knowledge and creativity.

Example Prompts:

1. Dialogue Creation:

Prompt: "Write a dialogue between a curious child and a wise old tree in an enchanted forest. The child is asking about the history of the forest, and the tree shares ancient secrets."

Why it Works: The prompt specifies the characters and setting, guiding the AI to create a coherent and engaging dialogue. It can be adapted by changing the characters or the context.

2. Descriptive Passage (Internet-Connected):

Prompt: "Write a vivid description of a futuristic cityscape at dusk, incorporating elements of advanced technology and eco-friendly architecture. Include recent trends in sustainable urban development."

Why it Works: This prompt provides a clear setting and theme, leveraging internet connectivity to include current trends, ensuring the description is both imaginative and relevant.

3. Multimedia Script:

Prompt: "Create a script for a short animated film about a young inventor who creates a robot companion. The script should include dialogue, scene descriptions, and emotional moments."

Why it Works: The prompt outlines the structure and content, guiding the AI to produce a well-rounded and emotionally engaging script. It can be adapted for different genres or themes.

Travel Blog Entry (Internet-Connected):

Prompt: "Write a travel blog entry about a recent trip to Kyoto, Japan. Include descriptions of historic sites, cultural experiences, and practical travel tips based on recent travel trends."

Why it Works: This prompt specifies the format and content, leveraging internet connectivity to provide up-to-date travel tips, ensuring the blog entry is informative and engaging.

4. Fantasy Story:

Prompt: "Write the opening chapter of a fantasy novel where a young hero discovers he has magical powers. The setting is a medieval kingdom with dragons, wizards, and ancient prophecies."

Why it Works: The prompt provides a clear setting and plot elements, guiding the AI to create an intriguing and immersive opening chapter. It can be adapted by changing the setting or the central conflict.

Conclusion: Creating effective prompts for generating different creative text formats involves specifying the format, content, and context. By leveraging GPT-4's creativity and, where applicable, its internet connectivity, you can produce engaging and innovative content for various purposes. Whether creating dialogues, descriptive passages, multimedia scripts, travel blog entries, or fantasy stories, this approach ensures that your creative outputs are rich, detailed, and captivating. Using GPT-4 for creative writing not only enhances your projects but also sparks new ideas and inspirations.

8.15 Writing Different Kinds of Lists

Lists are a versatile tool used in various contexts, from organizing information to creating content for articles, presentations, and more. GPT-4 can assist in generating different kinds of lists, ensuring they are comprehensive and relevant. This section will guide you on how to craft effective prompts for generating various types of lists, leveraging GPT-4's ability to organize and present information clearly.

Example Prompts:

1. Top 10 Tourist Attractions:

Prompt: "Create a list of the top 10 tourist attractions in New York City, including brief descriptions of each attraction and why it's popular."

Why it Works: This prompt specifies the location and type of list, guiding the AI to generate a well-organized and informative list. It can be adapted for different cities or types of attractions.

2. Packing Checklist (Internet-Connected):

Prompt: "Generate a packing checklist for a week-long camping trip in the mountains, including essential gear, clothing, and safety items. Use recent trends in camping gear."

Why it Works: The prompt outlines the context and specifics of the list, leveraging internet connectivity to include up-to-date trends, ensuring the checklist is relevant and comprehensive.

3. Steps for Starting a Business:

Prompt: "List the steps for starting a small business, from the initial idea to launching the business. Include key considerations and tips for each step."

Why it Works: This prompt provides a clear goal and structure, guiding the AI to generate a detailed and practical list. It can be adapted for different types of businesses or industries.

4. Healthy Eating Tips:

Prompt: "Create a list of 10 tips for healthy eating, focusing on simple and actionable advice for maintaining a balanced diet."

Why it Works: The prompt specifies the topic and type of advice, ensuring the AI produces a list that is useful and easy to follow. It can be adapted for different health and wellness topics.

5. Must-Read Books (Internet-Connected):

Prompt: "Compile a list of must-read books for 2024, including a mix of fiction, non-fiction, and genres. Provide brief descriptions and why each book is recommended."

Why it Works: The prompt asks for a curated list with descriptions, leveraging internet connectivity to include the latest recommendations, ensuring the list is current and diverse.

Conclusion: Using GPT-4 to generate different kinds of lists involves crafting prompts that specify the context, content, and type of list needed. By leveraging the AI's organizational skills and internet connectivity, you can create comprehensive and relevant lists for various purposes. Whether it's for tourist attractions, packing checklists, business steps, healthy eating tips, or book recommendations, this approach ensures that your lists are well-structured and informative. Utilizing GPT-4 for list creation enhances your ability to organize and present information effectively, making it a valuable tool for both personal and professional use.

8.16 Keeping Track of Information

Efficiently tracking information is crucial for managing projects, personal tasks, and data organization. GPT-4 can assist in generating structured formats to keep track of various types of information, making it easier to manage and retrieve data. This section will explore how to craft effective prompts for keeping track of information, ensuring the AI helps create clear and organized outputs.

Example Prompts:

1. Project Management Tracker:

Prompt: "Create a project management tracker for a software development project, including sections for tasks, deadlines, responsible team members, and progress status."

Why it Works: This prompt specifies the project type and the necessary sections, guiding the AI to produce a comprehensive and organized tracker. It can be adapted for different types of projects.

2. Personal To-Do List (Internet-Connected):

Prompt: "Generate a weekly to-do list for managing household chores and personal tasks, including priorities and deadlines. Include tips for effective time management."

Why it Works: The prompt outlines the context and specifics, leveraging internet connectivity to provide up-to-date time management tips, ensuring the to-do list is practical and useful.

3. Meeting Notes Organizer:

Prompt: "Create a template for organizing meeting notes, including sections for the meeting date, attendees, agenda items, discussion points, and action items."

Why it Works: This prompt specifies the format and key sections, guiding the AI to produce a clear and structured meeting notes organizer. It can be adapted for different types of meetings.

4. Expense Tracker (Internet-Connected):

Prompt: "Develop an expense tracker for a small business, including categories for different types of expenses, amounts, dates, and payment methods. Use recent best practices for expense management."

Why it Works: The prompt outlines the necessary details and leverages internet connectivity to include best practices, ensuring the expense tracker is thorough and relevant.

5. Research Data Log:

Prompt: "Create a research data log template for tracking experimental results, including sections for the date, experiment description, variables, results, and observations."

Why it Works: This prompt specifies the format and key sections, guiding the AI to produce a detailed and organized data log. It can be adapted for different types of research projects.

Conclusion: Creating effective prompts for keeping track of information involves specifying the context, content, and format needed. By leveraging GPT-4's organizational capabilities and internet connectivity, you can generate structured and practical templates for various tracking needs. Whether for project management, personal to-do lists, meeting notes, expense tracking, or research data logs, this approach ensures that your information is well-organized and easily accessible. Utilizing GPT-4 for information tracking enhances your ability to manage and retrieve data efficiently, making it a valuable tool for both personal and professional use.

8.17 Writing Conversational Scripts

Creating conversational scripts is essential for applications such as chatbots, virtual assistants, and interactive voice response (IVR) systems. GPT-4 can assist in generating engaging and coherent conversational scripts tailored to various scenarios. This section will explore how to craft effective prompts for writing conversational scripts, ensuring the AI produces natural and contextually appropriate dialogues.

Example Prompts:

1. Customer Support Chatbot:
Prompt: "Write a conversational script for a customer support chatbot that helps users troubleshoot common issues with their internet connection. Include greetings, diagnostic questions, troubleshooting steps, and closing remarks."

Why it Works: This prompt specifies the scenario and key elements of the conversation, guiding the AI to create a coherent and helpful script. It can be adapted for different types of customer support scenarios.

2. Virtual Assistant for Appointment Scheduling:

Prompt: "Generate a conversational script for a virtual assistant that helps users schedule medical appointments. Include greetings, appointment details collection, confirmation, and rescheduling options."

Why it Works: The prompt outlines the context and structure of the conversation, ensuring the AI generates a script that covers all necessary aspects of appointment scheduling. It can be adapted for various types of scheduling needs.

3. Interactive Voice Response (IVR) System (Internet-Connected):

Prompt: "Create an IVR script for a bank's customer service line that assists customers with checking account balances, transferring funds, and reporting lost cards. Include menu options, prompts, and responses based on recent banking trends."

Why it Works: This prompt specifies the IVR context and leverages internet connectivity to incorporate current trends, ensuring the script is up-to-date and relevant. It can be adapted for different IVR applications.

4. E-commerce Product Recommendations:

Prompt: "Write a conversational script for an e-commerce chatbot that recommends products based on user preferences and browsing history. Include greetings, questions about preferences, product suggestions, and follow-ups."

Why it Works: The prompt outlines the flow of the conversation and key elements, guiding the AI to generate a personalized and engaging script. It can be adapted for different e-commerce scenarios and product types.

5. Health and Wellness Coach:

Prompt: "Generate a conversational script for a virtual health coach that provides users with personalized fitness and nutrition advice. Include initial assessments, goal setting, advice, and motivational support."

Why it Works: This prompt specifies the context and structure, ensuring the AI produces a comprehensive and supportive script. It can be adapted for various health and wellness topics.

Conclusion: Creating effective prompts for writing conversational scripts involves specifying the scenario, context, and structure of the conversation. By leveraging GPT-4's natural language processing capabilities and, where applicable, its internet connectivity, you can generate engaging and contextually appropriate dialogues for various applications. Whether for customer support, virtual assistants, IVR systems, e-commerce, or health coaching, this approach ensures that your conversational scripts are natural, helpful, and user-friendly. Utilizing GPT-4 for writing conversational scripts enhances the user experience and improves the effectiveness of your interactive systems.

8.18 Coming Up with Conversation Starters

Creating engaging conversation starters can be challenging, whether for networking events, social gatherings, or online interactions. GPT-4 can assist in generating a variety of conversation starters that are interesting and appropriate for different contexts. This section will explore how to craft effective prompts for generating conversation starters, ensuring the AI produces engaging and contextually relevant suggestions.

Example Prompts:

1. **Networking Event:**

Prompt: "Generate 10 conversation starters for a networking event in the tech industry. The starters should be professional yet engaging, encouraging discussions about current trends and innovations."

Why it Works: This prompt specifies the context and desired tone, guiding the AI to produce relevant and engaging conversation starters suitable for a professional setting. It can be adapted for different industries or event types.

2. Social Gathering (Internet-Connected):

Prompt: "Create a list of 10 conversation starters for a casual social gathering. Include topics related to recent movies, popular books, and trending social media topics."

Why it Works: The prompt outlines the context and leverages internet connectivity to include current trends, ensuring the conversation starters are timely and engaging. It can be adapted for various social settings.

3. Online Dating:

Prompt: "Generate 10 conversation starters for an online dating app that are light-hearted and help break the ice. Include questions about hobbies, travel experiences, and favorite movies."

Why it Works: This prompt specifies the setting and desired tone, guiding the AI to create conversation starters that are casual and effective for initiating online conversations. It can be adapted for different dating app scenarios.

4. Team-Building Activities:

Prompt: "Create a list of 10 conversation starters for team-building activities at a corporate retreat. The starters should encourage team members to share personal interests and professional experiences."

Why it Works: The prompt specifies the context and objectives, ensuring the AI generates conversation starters that foster team bonding and engagement. It can be adapted for various team-building contexts.

5. Classroom Discussions:

Prompt: "Generate 10 conversation starters for a high school classroom discussion on environmental issues. The starters should encourage students to share their thoughts and ideas on sustainability and conservation."

Why it Works: This prompt outlines the context and topic, guiding the AI to produce conversation starters that are educational and thought-provoking. It can be adapted for different classroom subjects and age groups.

Conclusion: Creating effective prompts for generating conversation starters involves specifying the context, desired tone, and topics of interest. By leveraging GPT-4's creativity and, where applicable, its internet connectivity, you can generate a variety of engaging and contextually relevant conversation starters for different scenarios. Whether for networking events, social gatherings, online dating, team-building activities, or classroom discussions, this approach ensures that your conversation starters are interesting and effective in initiating meaningful interactions. Utilizing GPT-4 for creating conversation starters enhances your ability to engage with others and facilitate enjoyable and productive conversations.

8.19 Writing Different Kinds of Marketing Copy

Effective marketing copy is essential for capturing the audience's attention and conveying the value of a product or service. GPT-4 can assist in generating various types of marketing copy, from product descriptions and social media posts to email campaigns and ad copy. This section will explore how to craft effective prompts for writing different kinds of marketing copy, ensuring the AI produces persuasive and engaging content.

Example Prompts:

1. **Product Description:**

Prompt: "Write a compelling product description for a new eco-friendly water bottle. Highlight its features, benefits, and sustainability aspects."

Why it Works: This prompt specifies the product and key selling points, guiding the AI to produce a detailed and persuasive description. It can be adapted for different products and features.

2. **Social Media Post (Internet-Connected):**

Prompt: "Create a series of three engaging social media posts to promote a flash sale on a fashion e-commerce website. Include hashtags, a call-to-action, and mention any current fashion trends."

Why it Works: The prompt outlines the context and elements to include, leveraging internet connectivity to incorporate current trends, ensuring the posts are timely and effective. It can be adapted for different sales or promotions.

3. Email Marketing Campaign:

Prompt: "Generate an email marketing campaign for a new online course on digital marketing. Include a subject line, introductory paragraph, course highlights, and a call-to-action."

Why it Works: This prompt specifies the components of the email, guiding the AI to produce a coherent and persuasive campaign. It can be adapted for different courses or products.

4. Ad Copy for Google Ads:

Prompt: "Write a set of three ad copies for Google Ads promoting a home workout app. Focus on the convenience, variety of workouts, and introductory offer. Ensure each ad is within the character limit."

Why it Works: The prompt outlines the key selling points and constraints, ensuring the AI produces concise and persuasive ad copy. It can be adapted for different apps or services.

5. Landing Page Content (Internet-Connected):

Prompt: "Create the content for a landing page promoting a new vegan meal delivery service. Include an attention-grabbing headline, key benefits, customer testimonials, and a call-to-action. Use recent industry statistics to support the claims."

Why it Works: This prompt specifies the structure and elements to include, leveraging internet connectivity to incorporate recent statistics, ensuring the content is compelling and credible. It can be adapted for different services or products.

Conclusion: Creating effective prompts for writing different kinds of marketing copy involves specifying the product or service, key selling points, and desired elements. By leveraging GPT-4's persuasive writing capabilities and, where applicable, its internet connectivity, you can generate a variety of engaging and effective marketing content. Whether for product descriptions, social media posts, email campaigns, ad copy, or landing pages, this approach ensures that your marketing copy is persuasive, timely, and tailored to your audience. Utilizing GPT-4 for marketing copywriting enhances your ability to attract and retain customers, driving successful marketing campaigns.

8.20 Proofreading and Editing Text

Proofreading and editing are crucial steps in ensuring that written content is clear, error-free, and professional. GPT-4 can assist in identifying and correcting grammatical errors, improving sentence structure, and enhancing overall readability. This section will explore how to craft effective prompts for proofreading and editing text, ensuring the AI provides valuable suggestions for improving your content.

Example Prompts:

1. **Grammar and Spelling Check:**

Prompt: "Proofread the following paragraph for grammatical errors and spelling mistakes. Correct any issues you find."

Text: The quick brown fox jumps over the lazi dog. It's a bright sunny day, and the birds are chirping melodously in the background.

Why it Works: This prompt specifies the task and provides the text, guiding the AI to identify and correct grammatical errors and spelling mistakes. It can be adapted for different lengths and types of text.

2. **Improving Readability (Internet-Connected):**

Prompt: "Edit the following email to improve readability and clarity. Ensure the tone remains professional and friendly. Include any necessary corrections for grammar and sentence structure."

Text: Dear Mr. Johnson, I hope your well. I am writing to inform you about the upcoming meeting scheduled on next Friday. We will discuss the project updates and review the progress made so far. Please let me know if you need any additional information before the meeting.

Why it Works: The prompt outlines the task and objectives, leveraging internet connectivity to ensure the editing is up-to-date with current language usage trends, enhancing readability and clarity.

3. Enhancing Flow and Structure:

Prompt: "Edit the following essay to enhance its flow and structure. Ensure that each paragraph transitions smoothly to the next and that the overall argument is coherent and well-supported."

Text: Climate change is a significant challenge facing our world today. Many factors contribute to this phenomenon, including greenhouse gas emissions and deforestation. One of the major consequences of climate change is the rise in global temperatures. In addition, it can lead to more frequent extreme weather events.

Why it Works: This prompt specifies the goal of improving flow and structure, guiding the AI to enhance the coherence and support of the argument. It can be adapted for different types of essays or articles.

4. Refining Style and Tone (Internet-Connected):

Prompt: "Edit the following blog post to refine its style and tone, making it more engaging and conversational. Correct any grammatical errors and awkward phrasing."

Text: Traveling is a wonderful experience that allows you to see new places and meet new people. It broadens your horizons and gives you a fresh perspective on life. However, it can also be stressful if not planned properly.

Why it Works: The prompt outlines the desired style and tone, leveraging internet connectivity to include current trends in blog writing, ensuring the text is engaging and well-polished.

5. Consistency and Accuracy Check:

Prompt: "Proofread the following technical document for consistency and accuracy. Ensure that all terms are used correctly and that the information is presented clearly and logically."

Text: The system architecture consists of three main components: the user interface, the application logic, and the database. The User Interface provides the means for users to interact with the system. Application logic handles the business rules and processes. Finally, the Database stores all relevant data.

Why it Works: This prompt specifies the task of checking for consistency and accuracy, guiding the AI to ensure that the technical terms and information are clear and logically presented. It can be adapted for different types of technical documents.

Conclusion: Creating effective prompts for proofreading and editing text involves specifying the task, providing the text, and outlining the desired improvements. By leveraging GPT-4's language processing capabilities and, where applicable, its internet connectivity, you can generate valuable suggestions for improving the clarity, coherence, and professionalism of your content. Whether for grammar and spelling checks, improving readability, enhancing flow and structure, refining style and tone, or ensuring consistency and accuracy, this approach ensures that your written content is polished and effective. Utilizing GPT-4 for proofreading and editing enhances your ability to produce high-quality, error-free text, making it a valuable tool for writers and editors.

About the Author

My passion for technology began in my youth when I first encountered the transformative power of computers. Over the years, my career has taken me through diverse fields, but my deep-seated love for technology has always drawn me back, especially with the rapid advancement of artificial intelligence. Since the public release of ChatGPT in November 2022, I have immersed myself deeply in this revolutionary tool, quickly mastering the nuanced art of AI prompt crafting.

In "Unlock the Power of Advanced AI Prompts: A Complete Guide," I share the insights and techniques I've developed to help you harness the potential of AI in your own endeavors. This guide is meticulously designed for tech enthusiasts, AI hobbyists, software developers, content creators, and educators—equipping you with the essential tools to effectively integrate AI into your projects.

My aim with this guide is to demystify complex AI concepts in a clear and practical manner, making advanced AI techniques accessible to a broad audience. Whether you are just starting out or looking to enhance your existing skills, I provide invaluable guidance on how to creatively and efficiently utilize ChatGPT prompts to achieve remarkable results.

Through this book, I strive to empower you to explore the transformative power of AI, unlock its full potential, and elevate your technological skills to new heights. Join me on this exciting journey and discover how advanced AI prompts can revolutionize your projects and ideas.

.

www.ingramcontent.com/pod-product-compliance
Lightning Source LLC
LaVergne TN
LVHW051331050326
832903LV00031B/3484